VILLENEUVE

WINNING IN STYLE

GERALD DONALDSON, who collaborated with Jacques Villeneuve on this book, is the author of the best-selling biography of Jacques' late father Gilles Villeneuve which has been critically acclaimed as the best book about a racing driver ever written. His biography of the late World Champion James Hunt has enjoyed similar success. The author of several other books, Gerald is also a highly respected Formula 1 journalist and commentator for the international media

VILLENEUVE
WINNING IN STYLE

Jacques Villeneuve
WITH Gerald Donaldson

CollinsWillow
An Imprint of HarperCollinsPublishers

First published as
Villeneuve: My First Season in Formula 1 in 1996 by
CollinsWillow
an imprint of HarperCollins*Publishers*
London

Revised paperback edition published in 1997

3 5 7 9 8 6 4 2

A CIP catalogue record for this book
is available from the British Library

ISBN 0 00 218767 1

Produced under license from Goldstar Holdings Corporation

The face, name and helmet of Jacques Villeneuve
are protected internationally by trademarks

Colour reproduction by Saxon Photolitho, Norwich
Printed in Great Britain by
Caledonian International Book Manufacturing, Glasgow

Contents

Racing Life

*One of the questions I get asked most often is
what it means to be the son of Gilles Villeneuve.
First of all, I am really proud of my father, and
no matter how much success I have as a driver,
it will never diminish his accomplishments or
what his memory means to F1 fans.*

Because of my father, I was born into a racing environment and it felt like a normal world to me. And after he was killed, in 1982, I became interested in speed for myself. I was only 12 years old then and I loved going fast on skis or on a motocross bike, and soon I wanted to race cars. But I've never wanted to follow in his footsteps. That's not the reason I'm doing it. I'm racing for myself. I haven't many memories of watching my father race, but I know he was one of the most exciting drivers because of his spectacular style. We went with him on most race weekends and lived in a motorhome in the paddock. I was usually playing with my toy racing cars and didn't pay much attention when he was out on the track.

I do remember the way he was outside of racing. He would go out in his 4x4 truck and try to climb up mountains, or be speeding in his boat on the Mediterranean, or on a snowmobile in the winter. He would always go like crazy and I'm sure that he drove his Ferrari the same way as when he was having fun with his toys.

My father's reputation certainly helped get my racing career started, but it also put a lot more pressure on me because people compared us all the time. When most drivers start racing nobody knows who they are until they make a name for themselves. But when you start racing with a name like mine, everybody knows who you are and they are expecting you to succeed. Maybe those expectations and that extra pressure helped my progression as a driver because I had to work harder. I will never know because that's the only way it's ever been.

Racing has helped me learn lessons about life. One of them is that you're bound to make mistakes. It's so important to learn from your mistakes, not only in racing, but in anything you do. I think it's a big key to success in anything. If you make a mistake you should avoid making it again, but you shouldn't dwell on it or you'll make yourself miserable. The important thing is to be happy. It's silly to force yourself to do things that make you unhappy. There's no point in it. If you know what makes you happy you should do it.

It doesn't take much to make me happy. Success on the race track helps but, basically, just being normal and doing normal things is a source of happiness. Being with my girlfriend, going out for dinner, bowling or playing pool with friends. Accomplishing something makes me happy, but so does just relaxing, reading, playing on my computer. I'm still a kid at heart and that will never change.

Music is very important to me. I have a big collection of CDs and love listening to them. I would rather do that than watch TV. I used to play the trumpet but now it's mostly the piano. I like nice melodies. I didn't used to listen to the words of songs but I do now and often the words are so stupid. What I like are lyrics that mean something and music that really grabs you, almost puts you in a trance. You can close your eyes, bring back memories, feel emotion and be transported into another world.

I've tried writing my own lyrics, mostly when I was racing in Japan. I was by myself a lot and things would go on in my mind when I was trying to fall asleep. I would mull things over, think of some words to describe it, write them down and then put them to music. But I don't have much time to do this now.

I read a lot, especially books like 'Lord of the Rings' by Tolkien and science fiction books. I don't want to read about something that happens every day. I want to escape into

BORN TO RACE

Racing is not like a gene that you can inherit. But when you come from a family where racing was always there, you get used to speed at an early age.

something that's completely unreal, but makes sense when you put yourself into that other world, and I like that.

In the real world racing has taken me to many places, but I feel most at home in Europe, especially Monaco where we moved when I was six years old. I spent six years in boarding school in Switzerland and lived and raced in Italy, Japan and the States. But I also love going back to Canada, where I was born. It's where I spent all my summer holidays after we moved to Europe. So it seems more like my summer camp in a way. But I feel Canadian. I will always be Canadian, not only by birth. That's the way I feel inside. Our Quebec heritage has always been very strong at home. And I think it's important that you keep your roots like that.

I'm very close to my mother and my sister Melanie, and that's why I'm lucky because, besides being family, we're the best friends in the world. That's very important to me. My manager Craig Pollock has become a great friend. And I've always been close to my racing teams. I think it's important in a working relationship to have a good rapport and it's easier to do that if you can become friends.

I am also very close to my girlfriend, Sandrine Gros D'Aillon. We have similar backgrounds. She's from Montreal and she lived 10 years in Monaco, where we met. Of course, with my racing and her being at university in Montreal we don't see each other as often as we want. But she comes to the races whenever she can. I believe it's important to have someone that you can rely on, and you can feel their support and that they're behind you. That's a big help in racing, and in life.

I prefer people who are genuine and try to be that way myself. I don't believe in being nice to someone you don't necessarily like just because you want to get something from them. Life is not just business and making money, though the more you can get the better, and I certainly like spending it! But a lot of people think success is only making more money and they will say 'Yes' to anybody and smile at anybody, and invite people they dislike over to dinner, and do it as if they were friends. I hate that.

Another thing, which you often see in racing, is when people crash together and though one of them obviously made a mistake the other guy won't blame him. He tries to be diplomatic, but he should say: 'I think what he did is stupid.' On the other hand, if you make a mistake yourself you should admit it. Humanity makes itself unnecessarily complicated by

FUTURE CONSIDERATIONS

In school I was interested in math and physics and could have gone in that direction for a career. But I would have needed some kind of competition in my life. I might have gone ski racing, but chose cars instead. Later on, it would really interest me to do something in computers or music.

not telling it like it is. That's why I say be genuine. Be someone who says what he thinks.

MOVING TO F1

In 1994, my first season in IndyCars, there had been talks with several of the top F1 teams. After my good results in 1995, especially after winning the Indy 500 in May, the talks became more serious, particularly with Williams, and my manager Craig Pollock also had offers for me from other teams. But before making a decision to move to F1 I wanted to know what an F1 car was like to drive, and because the IndyCar season finishes relatively early I had to know soon whether a move would be likely. So, in August, when we were given the opportunity to test a Williams Renault at Silverstone it was a perfect situation. I was able to learn about F1 by testing the best car.

I was happy with the lap times right away and felt quite comfortable in the car. That took away a big question mark in my mind. And the Williams people were great. They wanted the test to go well and were very helpful. We struck up a good short term relationship and I had a lot of fun during those three days.

There were three factors influencing our decision to go F1 racing with the Rothmans Williams Renault team. First of all, it was a top team, with one of the best cars, and I had enjoyed driving it. Also, the people on the team were accustomed to success, they had made me feel welcome and it looked like we could get along well together.

The second factor was the timing of the Williams offer. I wanted to be able to make the decision quickly so I could go back to concentrating on the rest of the IndyCar season. The door was open, the opportunity was there and I had to take it before the door closed again. It was the time of year when all the top F1 drivers were looking for drives, and also the time for me to renew my IndyCar options.

The third reason we chose Williams was because it was the best offer for my future. The contract was for more than one year, which is important because you could always have a bad year, the car might be wrong the first year, and so on. So the security was important.

It was difficult to leave Team Green, my IndyCar team. The three years we spent together had been great. We worked well as a team, had our share of success, and there was a great deal of friendship among us. But everybody has to move on. You have to make your own life and take the better opportunities as they come along.

READY TO RACE

As a racing driver I've never been content to accept anything less than being able to challenge to win. This was my approach in the IndyCar series in America, where I managed to win several races, including the 1995 Indianapolis 500, and, at 24, I became the youngest IndyCar champion. A large part of the reason for that success was being well prepared, including doing as much testing as possible.

After signing with Williams in the fall of 1995 I did over 8,000 kilometres of testing to get ready for the 1996 season. In the beginning I had to become accustomed to the differences between an IndyCar and an F1 car. An F1 car is slower on the straights but much quicker in the corners. The engine has less horsepower but the power comes on quicker, and because an F1 car is lighter and more responsive it reacts faster to the driver's input, and the braking is much better.

The electronic gearchanging makes your life easier because you don't have to take your hand off the wheel and you can concentrate more on driving. F1 engines are another thing you don't have to worry about as much as in an IndyCar, where you have to deal with the delayed response of the turbocharged engines.

Because of its extra weight an IndyCar is a bit more physical to drive, it slides more easily and it's harder work to hold it. An F1 car is more twitchy and when it slides you have to react faster to catch it. It has higher limits, but I find this really enjoyable.

"Frank Williams didn't sign up Jacques to be a good number two. He's hot property and he's shown why he can come into F1 and do a first-rate job."

DAMON HILL *(Williams Driver)*

At first, before I understood the Williams car, it was my own limit I was pushing. Once I adapted to it and started feeling as one with the car, I was able to push myself to its limits and that's when the fun began. One of the great pleasures of driving a racing car is reaching the limits: your own and the car's. I love the sense of control you get when you're really pushing it, so that you feel right on the edge and you keep it there, lap after lap.

Testing was one thing, racing would be another. In F1 racing I would still have to find out how the car reacts during a race, how much downforce it might lose in traffic, and so on. The standing starts would be new because IndyCar racing has rolling starts, the race strategy would be different because F1 doesn't have many pace car and yellow flag situations which bunch up the field, and the F1 pit stops would be about twice as fast.

One of the main tasks in my first F1 season would be to learn the new circuits. But I had to do that since I started racing because I moved to different series quite often, from Italy to Japan in Formula 3, then to North America, at first in Formula Atlantic and then IndyCars. With Williams I was also able to test on some of the Grand Prix tracks – Silverstone, Monza, Imola, Magny Cours, Barcelona and Estoril – and in the past I had raced at Suzuka, Montreal and Monaco, though in other types of cars.

Knowing the track is useful because you don't have to go through the process of discovering where to place the wheels in the corners, where to brake and so on, and you can concentrate on bringing the car up to speed, instead of yourself. I never had trouble adapting before, and in one way the new F1 regulation limiting qualifying to only one hour, on Saturday, could help me. On Friday, instead of having to qualify, I would be able to spend the time working on the car set-up.

I didn't expect F1 racing was going to be any tougher than IndyCar, where there is traditionally more wheel-to-wheel racing because the cars are mechanically more evenly matched. But I would have to learn about the F1 drivers, how they behaved in various racing situations, who you could trust in a close fight and so on. I think my reputation is for driving hard and fair, and I hoped that those I would be competing against would be the same way.

I had heard F1 had a reputation for being cold, tough, ruthless and unfriendly. The drivers were supposed to be like robots, or puppets with people pulling their strings in all directions, and there was supposed to be no life within the teams. From my first impressions I was pleased to find that this was not correct. It seemed more like a big family and I was happy to be part of it. I was made to feel very welcome, especially in the Williams team.

From the beginning I got along well with my new team mate Damon Hill and did not expect we would have any problems during the season. I would not have come to F1 if I only had the opportunity to be second, and there were to be no team orders so we would both be trying to win.

Over the winter our lap times in testing were always competitive, but after testing so much you get a bit tired of just going around and around alone and you need the stimulation of actual competition. By the end of the year I was really eager to get into the racing mode.

CHAPTER TWO

AUSTRALIAN GRAND PRIX

MELBOURNE, AUSTRALIA, 10 MARCH 1996

It ended in disappointment, but there was the consolation of having had an almost perfect weekend in Australia. I started my first Formula 1 Grand Prix from pole position, led most of the way, set the fastest lap in the race and finally finished second. It was only disappointing because I came so very close to winning.

Before this race there were a lot of unknowns, for me and for everybody else. As a newcomer I was the focus of a lot of media attention, from many more journalists and photographers than at any time in my career. Not being familiar with the way the F1 media works on a race weekend and not knowing all the faces I felt a bit of a stranger.

But the reception wasn't negative. It had more to do with curiosity because I wasn't part of the establishment. People were aware of my successful IndyCar background and my competitive times in testing for Williams, but I still had to prove myself where it counted – in an F1 race – and there was the possibility I might fall flat on my face.

Sometimes all the attention, the press conferences, private interviews, public appearances, sponsor work, photo sessions and so on got pretty hectic and I found it hard to concentrate on racing. But this is part of the sport and you have to act professionally and keep smiling through all the distractions. It also helped that the first race of the season was in a pleasant environment.

I'm not really much of a sightseer but walking around the attractive city of Melbourne was enjoyable, as was the discovery that we would race in parkland near the centre of the city. Our hotel was right beside the circuit, so before it was closed to the public I jogged around it and also did some laps on roller blades. Besides helping to learn the circuit and become acclimatized to the heat, this was a good workout to help overcome the jet lag after the long journey to Australia.

I had no trouble sleeping at night, but whoever was in the hotel room next to mine might have had some unrest because of my guitar practice. At home in Monaco I play a bit of piano, but it's not very portable so my sister Melanie, who is studying music, suggested I should bring a guitar to Australia. Eventually, with the help of an instruction book, I was able to play a few chords, and by the end of the weekend my nightly guitar sessions were relaxing and fulfilling. Until then the learning process had been slow and somewhat frustrating, unlike the situation on the Melbourne circuit.

After our successful winter testing we knew the Rothmans Williams Renault team could be competitive at the start of the season, but, personally, I wasn't really expecting to be fighting for a win right away. My hopes were quite high, but I kept telling myself I still had a lot to learn about F1 and it would be unrealistic to think I could immediately be in front. But I was.

After being quickest on Thursday, in the special familiarization session laid on for everyone to learn the new circuit, we – my engineer Jock Clear and the rest of the guys

COMPARING CARS

If you put an IndyCar and an F1 car on the same road circuit the F1 would have a quicker lap time, probably about three or four seconds a lap quicker on a typical F1 circuit. The IndyCar might have a higher top speed, because it has more horsepower, but it would be slower around the corners. On an oval like Indianapolis the IndyCar should be faster, but on a trickier short oval like Phoenix I'm not sure which would be quicker because you could get a lot of cornering speed in the F1 car. It would be interesting to try it.

who work on my car – concentrated on getting the set-up right for qualifying on Saturday. In that one hour session there was a lot of traffic because there were 21 other cars fighting for grid positions. I really went for it, pushing as hard as I could, and even though we only had two clear laps, the quickest of them was good enough for pole position. At that point our expectations for the race escalated, but I was also apprehensive.

The standing start was something of an unknown factor because IndyCar racing has rolling starts. My last standing start experience was in Formula Atlantic racing in 1993, but those cars are smaller and F1 cars have three times the power. Also, in Atlantic and before that in F3, my starts were not really a strong point because I was too excited and nervous.

I also had some misgivings about the higher cockpit sides which F1 cars have to give the drivers better protection in side impact accidents. Your peripheral vision is somewhat impaired, as is your rear view through the mirrors, and it would be easy to lose sight of cars alongside and close behind, particularly when everyone is bunched together going into the first corner. As it turned out, no one was particularly close to me.

I got a perfect start, but then I saw the red flag and thought: 'Well shoot! I was fortunate to get one good start and now I'll have to do it all over again.' The first one might have been beginner's luck and that was unlikely to happen twice in a row. The race was stopped because of Martin Brundle's big accident, and it was reassuring to see that the safety measures worked and he was not hurt.

Waiting for the re-start I concentrated completely on relaxing. Sitting there on the grid you are in a different world.

RACING GEAR

In my racing gear Ann Bradshaw, the Williams team press officer, thinks I look like a midget American football player. I hope she is talking about my muscles! But it's true that my driving suit is oversized. It's for comfort in the cockpit because I hate having tight clothing. With the seatbelts done up you're already so confined you can hardly breathe. If your suit is pulling your arms or legs it can be very annoying sitting in the driver's seat for a two-hour race. Anyway, the clothes I wear regularly are oversized for better comfort. And it's the same with the driving suit. I don't really care what it looks like as long as it's comfortable. The design on my helmet is my own. When I started racing I took a piece of paper and a worked out a design and a colour scheme. There is a bit of a 'V' in the design but it wasn't really the idea behind it.

You're calmer than you've ever been. At least you try to be. You're forcing yourself to relax because it's very easy to become hyper. Only a few seconds separate you from success or failure. You have to forget about the pressure and say to yourself: 'It's only a race start, just be relaxed, look at the lights.'

You focus on the lights. When they go out the race is on. You do not blink. There is nothing else in your world. Just the lights, your eyes, your hands and your feet. When the lights go out you just let yourself go. You don't force it, you just let it happen.

As it happened I took the lead again and from the first lap my team mate Damon Hill was pressing me. He was very quick because, though our set-ups are quite different, our cars are basically the same. On some laps I would be quicker and get a small advantage and not push as hard. Then Damon would close up and I would have to do another quick lap to preserve the cushion. The gap between us was never much more than a second, and often less than that when we were lapping slower traffic.

"It was a big surprise to see him on pole in his first Grand Prix. This guy is really quick and talented"

NIKI LAUDA *(Three-time World Champion)*

The whole race went like that, a tight battle between the two of us and there was no let-up. This was great fun, really enjoyable. We fought hard and we fought fairly. I was happy about this because some F1 drivers have a reputation for not fighting cleanly.

After our pit stops for more fuel and fresh tyres Damon got in front of me. If I was to overtake him I knew it would have to be before his tyres got up to proper running temperature, so I closed right up on his gearbox. It was a fierce battle because he naturally kept the best racing line in the corners. In one of them he went wide and I had to go even wider. There was just enough room and I had just enough extra speed to get by him. It was very close, but very satisfying and for me it was the highlight of the race.

From then on the situation was the same as before, with Damon filling my mirrors and me working hard to stay in front. On one occasion I pushed a bit too hard and got sideways, bounced over a kerb and went off the circuit and on to the grass. It was always hairy at this particular corner, where it was very bumpy in the braking area and you risked spinning if you hit the brakes in the wrong spot. In the heat of the moment I braked where I shouldn't have and the rear end came loose and the car went sideways. I really thought I was going to lose it completely, but somehow managed to keep control.

Then came the problem over which I had no control. Coming past the Rothmans Williams Renault pit I caught a glimpse of a different message on the signalling board. It said 'SLOW', but I didn't understand why this should be, nor could I at first comprehend the bad news I was getting over the radio. A couple of laps later the message came loud and clear, from Jock Clear. He was screaming for me to slow down, otherwise I might not finish the race.

The telemetry information was showing a progressive loss of oil pressure in the engine. There was a major oil leak and the distinct possibility that my Renault engine could blow up. A couple of laps later the red light in the cockpit came on. The oil pressure was dropping fast. With just five laps to go I had no

AIMING HIGH

A realistic goal for my first F1 season would be to finish in the top three. But I am aiming at winning. If you want to achieve anything you've got to aim high.

option but to back off and let Damon go by.

I felt crushed. Everything suddenly became heavier, as if a great weight had descended on me. After fighting so hard and so well there was a tremendous letdown. To have victory in sight and then to have it taken away was devastating. So near, yet so far. But it's part of racing. When everything – the driver, car and engine – is pushed to the limit something can go wrong. The important thing now was to keep going and try to preserve second place points for the team.

In the last few laps I just concentrated on surviving to the finish, having to go slower and slower because in the corners the red light was coming on more and more, telling me there was less and less oil. In the end, it was fortunate the engine lasted because there was hardly any oil left.

It was only after the race that we found the oil leak was caused by damage to the undertray, which must have happened when I ran over a kerb. Normally, the car is strong enough to withstand this but in a way it was a relief to learn I was perhaps partly responsible. It made second place a little bit easier to take.

While it was still very annoying to have such a promising beginning come to such a frustrating ending, my first Formula 1 weekend was a success. For anyone who doubted it, my competitiveness proved that I was not out of place. For me, it was satisfying to achieve my goal: to be able to hold my own against the F1 establishment. But I knew there was still a lot to learn, and had I won my first race it might not have been an accurate reflection of this. Finishing second underlined the fact that there was room for improvement.

BRAZILIAN GRAND PRIX

SÃO PAULO, BRAZIL, 31 MARCH 1996

Every race of my first F1 season was to be a learning experience, and here the lesson was about racing in the rain. Quite a new test for me. In fact, my only previous wet-weather race was in an F3 car in Japan. But I learned a lot from this, my second F1 race, especially from the mistake that put me out before it was half over.

From Australia we flew directly to Brazil where we were looking forward to a relaxing holiday before the Grand Prix. The place where we stayed on the coast was very nice, a big house with miles of beaches right on the doorstep. The only problem was that there were always photographers and journalists waiting for us on the beach. It's hard to mind your own business when everybody else is trying to do it for you, and it was difficult to relax. To avoid the hassles Craig and I played tennis for three or four hours every day, so at least we got a good workout.

Then we moved into a hotel in São Paulo, a huge city with a lot of traffic. To avoid it we organized a helicopter to get to the circuit, but a couple of times bad weather prevented us from flying and it took over two hours to get back to the hotel. Away from the track there was also some business to attend to and it was all rather tiring and stressful.

Unlike the first race in Australia, where there was a separate day set aside for everyone to learn the new circuit, I had to learn the Interlagos track while the others were setting up their cars. This put us a bit behind on Friday, but once the track became familiar we were able to improve the set-up and quickly make up for the lost time. Before qualifying on Saturday we were close to the pace set by my team mate Damon Hill.

After setting a qualifying time which put me third on the grid, I felt there was more to come from the car and decided to try another quick lap, to get closer to Damon who was on pole. At the end of qualifying you have nothing to lose - you either do a quick lap or you go off. This time I went off, onto the grass, but it was worth trying because the computer showed up to that point it had been a quicker lap.

We made more changes to the car and were second fastest in the Sunday morning warm-up and optimistic about the race. The car felt strong and consistent in the new set-up, well-suited for what promised to be a long and tough Grand Prix. But it would also be a wet one, as everyone found out when a torrential downpour began a few minutes before the start. This changed the picture completely, for the cars which were set up for dry conditions and for me, with my lack of experience of racing in the rain.

I knew my wet weather F1 debut would have to come some time, so the sooner, the better. Before the start, while the guys were putting rain tyres on the car, I had no real strategy because there was almost nothing to base it on. We had one wet race in Japanese F3 in 1992 (where I finished fourth), and in two years of IndyCar racing we probably only did about a

THE F1 MEDIA

The media coverage of F1 is much bigger than in IndyCar racing and the people are a lot more aggressive. I thought I was prepared for this but I must admit that in Brazil, particularly, the pressure from photographers and journalists was unbelieveable. It started several days before the race and never let up. It was distracting and made it harder to concentrate on racing. But this is the price you pay to be in F1. Besides, it's a good sign when you've got the media interested in you. If you weren't doing well nobody would care.

dozen laps in the wet. In testing with Williams over the winter we had a couple of rainy days, but testing is quite different from racing.

On the way out to the starting grid there was a huge puddle of water where the car felt more like a boat, and I was worried I might crash in the pit lane. On the formation lap the car was aquaplaning everywhere and it all felt very hairy.

But the start went well enough and I even got ahead of Damon for a moment, but he immediately fought back and went into the lead. He told me later that after starting from pole there was no way he wasn't going to lead the first lap. I could understand that, because for the first few laps he was the only one who could see where he was going. Visibility for those following him was severely reduced by spray and I lost a huge amount of time.

It took a while to become acclimatized to the unfamiliar conditions, and trying to find the best racing lines in the rivers of water involved a lot of guesswork and experimentation. Every lap was different, and with the car sliding around so much and not being able to feel what it was doing I was on tip-toes. It was very tense.

After about five laps I was on Damon's pace, but by that time he was already well on the way to what turned out to be an excellent win for him and the team. The job now was to defend my second place against Jean Alesi, who is noted as one of the best wet weather drivers.

I was actually enjoying myself, sliding around while there was still a lot of water on the track surface. However, the rain began letting up and a dry racing line was gradually appearing, so it became more important to keep Jean behind until my pit stop, when a change to dry weather tyres would be ideal to take advantage of our car's set-up. At this time the track conditions were still about equally divided between wet and dry, and it was the difference that caught me out.

As we were lapping a slower car Jean was able to get alongside, and we went into the next corner together. On previous laps I had been taking this corner faster and faster as the racing line dried out and now I attempted to take it at the same speed, momentarily forgetting that I was on the wet part of the track. The grip was just not there and I spun off the track. My immediate reaction was to think: 'What an idiot!' I was really angry at myself because I made a stupid mistake.

"It's not as if Jacques has just come out of Formula 3. He's won the Indianapolis 500 and the IndyCar title. He's in control."
PATRICK HEAD *(Williams Technical Director)*

I hate making mistakes. To a certain extent it is inevitable when you're pushing a car to the limit. And even though it was easy to get caught out in these conditions, it was no excuse. I'm a paid professional, a championship winner, and I should be able to keep the car on the road, no matter what.

I could not get back across the track, so I spent the rest of the race sitting in a course marshal's truck. Luckily it had a television set and I watched until the end of the race. As a spectator it was enjoyable viewing. As a former participant it was miserable, especially when the track dried out. That was doubly annoying because our car would have been perfect for those conditions. But it was stuck in a gravel trap.

Back in the garage after the race when I apologized to the team they were suprisingly understanding. I expected them to be as annoyed as I was at needlessly throwing points away. I am sure it would be different if it was one of the last races and we were fighting for a position in the championship. But there were still 14 races to go and many more points at stake.

Also on the positive side, my negative result in the Brazilian Grand Prix furthered my education as an F1 driver. I learned more about racing in the rain which will no doubt be useful in the future, as will the lesson learned from spinning out of the race. Learning from mistakes is a personal objective, and this costly mistake was one I did not intend to repeat again. And I would not be dwelling on it. This race was history and I was already looking forward to trying to win next weekend, in Argentina.

THE LEARNING CURVE

When I started racing in 1988, in touring cars in Italy, I was just a kid fooling around and crashing often. I got more serious in the first year of Italian F3 and stayed on the road more. By the second year I was getting closer to the frontrunners. In the third year I was up with the frontrunners and just starting to fight with them.

One of the best ways to keep learning is to give yourself more challenges. At the end of the 1991 season I thought I needed a change, either to go into F3000 or to some other more competitive series. We didn't have enough sponsorship to compete on even terms with the top F3000 teams so there was no point in doing it half way.

Then, when I did the F3 races at Macao and Fuji, the Tom's Toyota team approached me to do the F3 series in Japan and I thought it was a good idea. Going to Japan would put me in a different culture, not just the country but in racing as well. There were some top drivers in the series who had a lot of experience, more than there were in Italy, and I would learn faster.

It was a risky move in some ways, but it proved to be a good one. I learned to work harder, which was a good thing because up until this point I was lazy! The Tom's team didn't speak much English so I had to work harder with the engineers. They put a lot more weight on my shoulders when it came to things like making decisions about the set-up and so on. All in all, the extra responsibility changed for the better my way of thinking and working.

The timing was right. Earlier, it wouldn't have been as good. It was my fourth year in F3 and I was more mature. In the races I learned a lot about tactics and strategy – how to think and plan ahead, to watch what was happening and to react to it – not just go balls-out on every lap.

It all came together logically and naturally. I think it's important that you're capable of learning by yourself, through your own experience. Someone else telling you what to do will help a bit, but you learn faster by yourself, either by making mistakes and correcting them or by seeing what's gone well and using that. That's what happened to me in Japan.

When I moved to Formula Atlantic racing in 1993 in North America, the cars were more fun to drive. They had bigger wheels than F3 cars, more downforce and a bit more horsepower, so you could throw them around. It was more like a go-kart with a lot of power.

The reason we chose the Atlantic series was to eventually move up to IndyCar racing. The year in Atlantic was mainly to get accustomed to the tracks, especially the ovals, to the different racing mentality, and so on. Also, going from F3 directly into IndyCars would have been a huge step – especially in power. The Atlantic cars were better training for this because they had a lot more grip than F3 cars, with ground effects similar to IndyCars.

When you go up the ladder in a series you have to work until it feels as natural as it did in the smaller series. The big thing was to get accustomed to all the power in an IndyCar. It took time to handle that. The first couple of days testing your heartbeat goes much higher than it normally does because everything happens so much quicker than you are used to.

It's not that it's scary, it's just that everything happens so fast. You're just shifting, braking, turning the wheel – all in a blur. You don't really know what's happening. After about five laps you're as tired as you've ever been in a racing car.

The cars are bigger and generate more downforce, so you have to be able to handle that, and in the races there is more turbulence because of the higher speeds and that took a lot of adjustment. You had to learn to get the most out of the turbo engine, allowing for the throttle lag especially, and also the huge acceleration when the power comes on.

The IndyCar pit stops were also a new thing; you don't have them in the smaller formulae, and running with 40 gallons of fuel changes the handling of the cars, so you have to adapt to that. In the smaller series the races are short, but in IndyCars you run for two hours or more, and sometimes for 500 miles at places like Indianapolis and Michigan. This requires a lot of stamina and you have to keep your concentration level up all the time. And on the short ovals you're in a total traffic jam for the whole race, so you need to learn about overtaking – which requires a lot of good judgement when you're going about 230 miles an hour a few inches from a cement wall!

The other big thing about the IndyCar series is that the competition level is very high because the cars are so evenly matched. In any race you could have a dozen cars capable of winning. There is a lot of wheel-to-wheel racing, and you have to learn to deal with traffic or you won't get anywhere. And don't forget, in IndyCar racing you have some of the best drivers in the world. F1 drivers get more publicity but the top IndyCar drivers are also very good.

All of us were on a learning curve because Team Green was also new to IndyCar racing. We worked really well together and kept making progress all the time. At the start of the 1994 season we were within a second of the leading lap times in qualifying. In the second half of the season we were within half a second, sometimes closer. We only needed that half-second and that came right away in 1995. We were always on the pace and got the pole six times, set the fastest race lap six times and won several races, including the Indy 500.

With that variety of past experience making the transition to F1 was not that difficult. But there was still a lot to learn, as I proved when I fell off the learning curve in Brazil.

ARGENTINE GRAND PRIX

BUENOS AIRES, ARGENTINA, 7 APRIL 1996

Finishing second was more satisfying than in Australia where, after leading nearly all the way, it was disappointing. Here the car worked well, and though a slow start meant it was necessary to fight hard to regain lost positions, this added to the pleasure and helped make up for my mistake in Brazil. With Damon winning again our team had a perfect weekend.

Coming here immediately after a very hectic week in Brazil gave us extra time to rest and relax, and the more leisurely build-up to the race paid off. We were able to examine the Buenos Aires circuit more thoroughly, lapping it slowly in a rental car so it required fewer laps to learn in the racing car. It was really more like a go-kart track, with many slow corners and hardly any straights between them. There were also a couple of severe bumps which in a racing car felt like an electric shock up your backside each time you ran over them. But none of the corners with their wide run-off areas gave that special feeling – the rush – you only get on faster corners where there is more risk of hitting something if you go over the limit.

The tight configuration of the track also lessened any mechanical advantages, so the field was bunched closer together and qualifying positions were important. The asphalt was quite slippery and therefore good for racing because you slide around more, which is fun, and it forces driving errors which you can take advantage of, providing you don't make them yourself. I made one on Saturday morning, sliding off the track and shortening my practice, but the qualifying session in the afternoon went well. Third on the grid (behind Damon and Michael Schumacher) after losing those laps in the morning was encouraging. We made more set-up improvements so that in the Sunday morning warm-up session the car felt good in race trim.

My start was terrible. The car got off the line well, but only for about a metre and then the engine hit the rev limiter. It seemed like there was a huge amount of wheelspin but actually it was the clutch slipping. I had somehow failed to release the clutch properly, the power came to the rear wheels about three seconds later than it should have and suddenly I was in ninth place.

In the first corner a front wheel took a hard hit from another car but no harm was done. Our chassis set-up was at its best with a full load of fuel so that inspired confidence for the battle to make up for lost time.

It was quite enjoyable overtaking several other cars in the first few laps. I passed two or three people at the entry to the same corner, moving up right behind them, then pulling out and braking later than they did. They were probably a bit surprised by this manoeuvre so they didn't have time to close the door. My extra speed meant a bit of wheel-locking and tyre-smoking under braking, but it was great fun to do, and probably to watch. The only problem was not many others saw it because the TV cameras were focused on the frontrunners. Anyway, it was satisfying to play catch-up.

We were up to fourth place by the time the first pit stops came around. The handling was not as good on the new set of tyres, so it might have been more difficult to catch the remaining three cars in front. But then the whole field closed up again when a couple of accidents brought out the safety car so the drivers could be attended to (fortunately they weren't hurt) and their cars removed from dangerous positions.

The appearance of a safety car is unusual in F1 racing, but it is a regular feature in IndyCar racing and I think it should be used more often in F1. It forces everyone to slow down so there is less risk of hitting disabled cars or the track marshals working on them. When you're racing for position the safety car can help some drivers and hinder others, but when it's used frequently it tends to balance out the benefits for everybody. When the field gets bunched up again it makes a new race for the spectators, and it can provide further interest by influencing the timing of pit stops and forcing a change in race strategies.

> *"The single most impressive thing about him was what a fighter he was. He's a real tiger in the cockpit."*
>
> JONATHAN PALMER
> *(BBC commentator and former F1 driver)*

The rest of the race was fairly straightfoward. Our pit stops worked to perfection and so did our car, on a day when only 10 finished. We benefited from the retirements of a couple of cars in front, and over the last few laps it was only necessary to maintain the comfortable lead over Jean Alesi, who was in third place. When you are able to ease up it actually becomes tougher because when you are concentrating hard you don't feel the aches and pains. Going over the bumps had taken a toll and long after the race my heels were numb from the pounding. But this was a small price to pay for another visit to the podium.

On the podium we celebrated by spraying the champagne, as is the custom. But when you've worked hard I think you also deserve a sip. The only problem was that mine went down my nose and I almost choked!

Second place here helped make up for my disappointment in Brazil, and with Damon winning again the Rothmans

Williams Renault team scored its second one-two finish in just three races. We hoped to have more days like this, though in the future I would be trying hard to reverse our positions.

SANDRINE

Argentina was the first F1 race that my girlfriend Sandrine attended. She often came to the IndyCar races and it was good to have her support again. For a driver it is important to have not only your team behind you but also the people closest to you.

Sandrine understands how I am during a race weekend and knows what I need. That doesn't mean she behaves differently, in fact the opposite is true. Having her there, being herself, is more like being at home. It provides a feeling of normality in what is often a very artificial environment.

During the days, when you're not in the car, you sometimes have a few minutes here and there and that's when it's good to have someone around who you know and trust and can talk to. With Sandrine, even for a few seconds, I can relax and maybe get a hug and kiss before I go back to work.

Most of the time at the races she reads a book. She doesn't really care much for racing. All she cares about is that I perform well and that I don't hurt myself. She wasn't happy when I moved to F1 because after Roland Ratzenberger and Ayrton Senna were killed she thought it was more dangerous than IndyCar racing. I haven't been able to change her mind about that and if something should go wrong, it's better that she should be there.

After a day at the track we can go out to eat and get away completely from racing. We might talk a bit about racing, but it's not the same as talking to a journalist. You don't have to worry that what you say may be misinterpreted or twisted around. With Sandrine it's more of a dialogue and you can open yourself up. She helps take away some of the stress, which I may not notice is there, but I'm sure it is.

AT HOME IN MONACO

Following the Argentine race we went home for a few days. Once you start getting as busy as I am you don't really care where you live, as long as it's not a hotel room. But you need a base somewhere that is natural and feels like home. A place for friends to come and visit and a space where you can follow your other interests away from racing. It's very important to feel comfortable in your home environment, because if you're not content in the place where you have your private time you won't be happy in many places.

I feel very comfortable living in Europe, with the different cultures and mentalities, the mix of languages and cuisines. It's also good to be in a society that's not as business-oriented as North America, where I lived for the past few years. In some ways it seems Americans love work more than life and the Europeans think the opposite. Work is important but so is time to relax and enjoy yourself. It helps when you have an attractive area to come home to, and the Cote d'Azur in the South of France is very beautiful. When I was growing up here I took it all for granted, but returning after having lived in other parts of the world makes you appreciate it more.

When I moved from the States back to Monaco before the start of the season I was looking for a flat that was quiet and easy to get to. The place I found has a good view of the harbour

OTHER INTERESTS

Sometimes you just have to get away from racing. That
doesn't mean you shut yourself away from the rest of
the world. It means you do something other than
racing. It's important to get away from whatever you do
for a living, so you can come back to it with a fresh
perspective. Being locked into any one thing for too
long can make you blind to everything around you.
When you get away it opens up your eyes and you see
things you couldn't see before.

and the sea from the balcony. There isn't much furniture, what
there is is fairly high tech and modern, and it will most likely
remain comparatively empty so the space will seem bigger.
There's no reason just to add stuff and make it overcrowded.

Sometimes the flat gets in a bit of a mess, with stuff all over
the floor, but eventually, when I can't find anything, it gets
tidied up again. I try to avoid being sloppy and feeling clean is
very important. I brush my teeth after I eat anything; even
when I'm driving I don't want to put my helmet on after lunch
before brushing my teeth.

The flat is not far from my mother's place, where I often
visit, to talk and also to get some good food. I can cook, pasta
mainly, but some people think it's not very edible. I am not a
morning person, but I force myself to wake up early because
you have to do it at the races, and when I'm at home I like to
make my own breakfast, accompanied by music from my CD
collection. I might have French toast, cereal, bacon and eggs

WAYS OF WINNING

You don't have to finish first to feel like a winner. If you fight your way through a race, attacking all the way and having wheel-to-wheel battles with other cars, you've won a personal battle, no matter where you finish. Winning is the most important thing, but it's not as big a thrill as pushing the limit and being on the edge. There is a moment of euphoria in winning, but it's not the same feeling. And if you dominate a race from start to finish there is no adrenaline rush. But you need both. If I didn't win I would get frustrated and if there were no thrills I would get bored. Because you're paid to win as a professional it takes some of the fun out of racing. If I'm go-karting with friends it's a huge blast because it doesn't matter if you spin out or lose. As an F1 driver you have to be more serious about winning. You have to put thrill-seeking in the background, or even avoid it.

and hot chocolate. After breakfast I usually stay in, listening to music, reading, playing with the computer, or talking on the phone.

It's amazing the amount of time you can spend with a phone glued to your ear. The only problem is people sometimes don't understand that when you get home you want to do the things you haven't done for a month or so, and you've only got a couple of days to do them. I enjoy talking to friends, but sometimes you just want to relax and maybe not talk at all, certainly not about racing.

In the afternoon I usually do some training, but I don't overdo it. If I spent six hours training every day I would probably go crazy. There are a few good places for jogging and roller-blading, on paths near the sea, and Monaco is quite practical to do sports. I play tennis, often with a friend, and there is a gym at the tennis club. But rather than mindlessly lifting weights or sitting on a bicycle in a gym I prefer exhausting myself playing tennis, or skiing, or doing other sports where you have to think. You're not just standing there for hours getting bored and you're using your mind while you're building up your body.

I might go out to lunch or dinner with friends, or for a drink. I enjoy a beer at night, sometimes even on a race weekend, but it's seldom more than one. I'm not much of a drinker, though there is no harm in letting yourself go once in a while. At night, though I usually want to go to bed about 10:00, it's often 2:00 in the morning before I get to sleep. I feel I have so much to do that I don't want to go to bed. I become so absorbed in music or reading or the computer that I lose track of time.

EUROPEAN GRAND PRIX

NÜRBURGRING, GERMANY, 28 APRIL 1996

It was a memorable moment, crossing the finish line as the winner of the European Grand Prix, a moment shared with all on the Williams Renault team who were waving and cheering from the pit wall. My first F1 win would not have been possible if anybody had made a mistake, and we all savoured the satisfaction of a job well done.

But the moment was fleeting, partly because the post-race activities – dashing up to the podium, being presented with the winner's trophy, getting sprayed with champagne, going to the press conferences, giving interviews in several languages, signing autographs, and so on – seemed nearly as hectic as the race.

The circumstances leading up to the European Grand Prix were ideal for a good result. After the experience of our first three races, where our competitiveness was proven and rewarded with two second place finishes, our confidence and expectations were high. So was our team spirit. The chemistry among the people involved is one of the most important factors in a successful racing team, and ours was getting better and better. The more rapport you have the more productive you become, and as our relationship developed my race engineer Jock Clear and the rest of the guys who work on our car felt we were really coming together as a unit. Following a very encouraging test in Spain, where we found some improvements which will improve progress later in the season, our mood before the fourth race was more positive than ever.

On a personal level it also felt good to be back in Europe and spend a few days at home in Monaco, where I had hardly been at all since the season began. My 25th birthday celebration (on the 9th of April), with my girlfriend and a few friends, was a quiet affair – just dinner and a few drinks then listening to music at home – because it could not interfere with the serious fitness training I needed to catch up on. Anyway, 25 is just another number. If the years were one month longer, I would only be 24 but still the same age.

I arranged to take piano lessons because though it's

pleasant to play by yourself, there is more enjoyment to be had when you study and learn more about it. I also managed to find all the components necessary to assemble my own computer. The owner of the computer shop said it would be difficult for someone who had never done it before, but when he found out I had it working within three hours he jokingly offered me a job!

But I already had a job and off we went to Germany. I was looking forward to seeing the original Nürburgring. It was THE Formula 1 circuit, the one where the great drivers made so much racing history, so it was disappointing to find it closed to traffic for the race weekend. My first look at the modern Nürburgring where we would race was on a motor scooter, but it was such a cold day I only managed three laps before having to stop because I nearly froze!

When I went to the track on Thursday, I forgot my pass and

THE WINNING FORMULA

In IndyCar racing, because we were all new to the series, the expectations weren't as high. I started IndyCar racing with a new team and a new car, and for me it was a big jump from Formula Atlantic. I came into F1 with a top team, a team that was already well-established, and with a good car with benchmark set-ups from the year before, and so on. There was probably more pressure to perform right away in F1. But it's not easy to become a winner in any good series, otherwise a lot more people would be doing it!

TRAFFIC TACTICS

When you're being closely followed by another car, you have to be very alert when you're lapping slower traffic. When those in front are slower you have to judge where to make your move. For instance, if you get too close to a slower car at the wrong spot going into a corner, you'll be too slow coming out of the corner. And that's when the guy coming behind you can get a run on you. Michael did this to me several times at the Nürburgring when we were lapping traffic, but I was able to hold him off.

had to persuade the guy at the gate to let me in. When I explained that I was a driver for the Williams team he wondered whether I drove a truck or a limo for Frank Williams. He thought an F1 driver should look bigger and older, and was astonished when somebody told him who I was. Some people might get upset at this kind of thing, but I'm happy not to be recognized and thought it was all quite funny.

Viewed from the cockpit of our Williams Renault, the track proved to be less complex than those in Brazil and Argentina. Aside from a couple of slightly more difficult corners, most of the track was fairly straightforward – just braking and turning, right/left and left/right – and with no bumps which was a pleasant change from the South American tracks. There were also places where opportunities to outbrake an opponent might arise, and all in all the new Nürburgring seemed well-suited for some good racing.

Because the learning process was shorter, we could begin setting up the car earlier. This, too, was becoming easier, because as we became more accustomed to working together as a team we had a better basis, mechanical and personal, from which to work each weekend. All in all, we began practice with quite a lot of confidence. Second place on the starting grid, beside my team mate Damon, was promising, and considering that our race setup was even better than the qualifying setup our prospects for the race were looking good.

Taking the lead at the start was made easier when Damon was slow to get away (he eventually finished fourth), and soon there was quite a gap back to the rest of the pack. Until Michael Schumacher arrived on the scene it was actually getting a bit boring, leading the race with no one close behind. I wasn't complaining about it, because it makes my job easier but it's more fun when you have to fight. For instance, if you're go-karting with friends and you're going around the track by yourself, you slow down and wait for them so you can have a battle.

I didn't have to slow down for Michael because he was

A JOB TO DO

Williams is a winning team with a winning car. Everything is there to win. And as a driver you're not paid to cruise around. You're paid to give it your best shot and you have to give it everything you have. Where the team and car is concerned, it's all there. So all I have to do is my job.

driving very hard. Performing in front of his home fans, he was particularly inspired and fought aggressively for the whole race. Because of our race setup the Williams Renault had a bit more top speed on the straights than Michael's Ferrari, but he could brake harder and corner faster, so that over a complete lap our cars were very evenly matched.

"Jacques drove a fantastic race, with no mistakes and there was no way for me to pass him. But we had a great race together, with very close fighting."

MICHAEL SCHUMACHER
(Defending World Champion)

Michael was seldom much more than a second behind, and when we were lapping traffic he was a lot closer than that. At times he was too close for comfort, but it was fun, though it would not have been much fun if he had managed to get ahead! I wasn't nervous or apprehensive about the responsibility of leading the race. If you are in second place you don't start worrying about making a mistake or the car breaking down, so why do it when you're in first place?

Having Michael sitting there in my mirrors and applying constant pressure, where any mistake would have enabled him to get by, certainly made it easier to maintain concentration. Handling such pressure, though the risks are higher, is much more satisfying than dominating a race by a wide margin.

Then came the moment of euphoria at the finish. It was great to be on the top step of the podium and to see all the guys on the team jumping around and being so ecstatic. It was also rewarding to hear the Canadian national anthem being played. Even though you're not really racing for your country, you're racing for yourself and your team, you still represent your country and I'm proud to represent Canada.

To win any race is a great feeling and to win my first Formula 1 race, especially so soon, was extra special. It was great for the team as well, because we had all worked hard to be competitive since the beginning of the season, and to become a winner in the fourth race made it all worthwhile.

After we came down from the podium, there were mob scenes with the press. People were pushing microphones and tape recorders into my face and becoming aggressive. When it gets that hectic there is an inclination to run for it, but there was no escape route. On the way out to the hotel there was a mad rush of fans. When there are reasonable numbers of them you're happy to stop and sign autographs, but when you get swarmed it becomes claustrophobic.

Other people were more excited than I was about my first F1 win. While they were watching it happen, I was sitting in the car doing what I get paid to do. You're not there just to try and do it, you're there to DO it. I was just doing my job.

THE WINNING FEELING

The thing about winning, as I learned in IndyCar, is that you get used to it and you want more. I had been content to make it to the F1 podium, but now anything less than a win would seem like second best.

And after winning – doing what you're supposed to – you shouldn't dwell on it for long, saying 'Oh, I'm brilliant! I won the race.' Because if you think like that when you win, you also have to think negatively when you lose or how stupid you are if you make a mistake in a race. In fact, making a driving error probably stays longer with me than a win, because you have to remember a mistake to be able to learn from it so as not to repeat it.

So I won. It happened, then it was over. Life goes on. You can't just look backwards. Our celebrations were short but sweet. Because of heavy traffic leaving the Nürburgring we missed our flight back to Monaco and could only get as far as Geneva. There, with Craig Pollock and Michael Aymon, a friend from Villars, we enjoyed a glass of wine and then began concentrating on the next race.

SAN MARINO GRAND PRIX

IMOLA, ITALY, 5 MAY 1996

I almost felt like laughing when my race ended a few laps before the San Marino Grand Prix did. After trouble on the first lap, dropping back to last place, fighting back into contention, then having to stop just before the finish – what else was there to do but treat it as a cruel joke.

I was really looking forward to racing at Imola. For the first time this season it was a track we knew, from pre-season testing in the Williams Renault and from three years of racing in the Italian Formula 3 series. And after winning the previous weekend at the Nürburgring our morale was high.

With such a short interval between race weekends there was only time to spend a few hours at home, pick up my girlfriend Sandrine who flew in from Canada, then drive to Imola. I like travelling by car, even when it takes longer than a plane. I hate the aggravation of flying: driving to the airport, parking, checking in, going through customs, waiting for your flight, arriving at the next airport, more customs, waiting for luggage, hiring a rental car, and so on.

In your own car you can avoid all this, and on the way to Imola the feeling of independence reminded me of the years when I always drove to the races in Italy. I love the country and speak Italian almost as well as English. French is my main language and I tend to think in French. But I read mostly in English because I learned to read that way and sometimes, even with Sandrine, we end up speaking English on certain subjects.

Our journey was very enjoyable. Sandrine and I talked, listened to music on CD's we brought with us, looked at the scenery, stopped for coffee and generally took it easy. I drive fairly carefully on public roads, especially when someone is with me, travelling not much over the speed limit. We made it from Monaco to Imola in about four hours.

On the circuit we quickly got up to speed in the Williams Renault. The familiarity with the track, knowing where the limit was as opposed to having to spend time finding it, meant we were on the pace from the beginning of practice. The track used to be much nicer, but now, except for a couple of interesting high-speed corners, the slow chicanes which were built to improve safety make it rather uninteresting to drive.

Qualifying was very close and competitive, which made it exciting for the fans and for us. Our battle with Michael Schumacher and Damon went right down to the last few minutes. On my final lap I really went for it but got a bit sideways in the last corner and lost a couple of tenths of a second and dropped to third on the starting grid. However, we knew we had a strong car and in the warmup it felt even better. I had a very good feeling about the race, but that good feeling didn't last long.

Our start might be described as average. But when the guys in front did not get away as quickly as some of those behind, it meant we were stuck in a traffic jam and had to lift off a bit. Going into the first corner I managed to outbrake Jean Alesi and get alongside him. We banged wheels a bit, but no harm was done and with better acceleration I was able to get slightly in front of him before the next corner.

Then Jean hit me again, from behind, and my car flew up in the air for a moment. His car's front wing must have cut a tyre, because about 300 metres further along it suddenly deflated. It was okay until I put pressure on the tyre when braking for a corner, and then it came off the wheel. This meant the car was a tricycle, and suddenly I found myself going off onto the grass. I got going again but there was no option but to stop at the pits.

This setback, having such a promising race short-circuited by such an incident, was very annoying. Jean and I had a chat about it later. Neither of us was happy about it because the

ON THE EDGE

I love the feeling when you're right on the edge and pushing it. The greatest pleasure is when you're going through a corner and the car gets very light, just short of sliding, and you hold it there. You're really on the limit, you can feel it, and you're controlling it. There is more pleasure when you manage to understand how the car is reacting, so that you can make changes to it and push the edge even further.

You wonder how far you can push it. You feel where you are in terms of balance, and you know it wouldn't take much to lose it and that every small movement you make affects what's happening. But you keep pushing and you know you're out there on the edge. Even by yourself it's a great feeling and when you set a quick lap time or you go around a corner quicker than the other guys you have proof you're doing something special.

When you've been out on the edge and you have time to think about it, you've got a huge grin on your face. You know you've done something special. Others might call it crazy, but for you it was controlled. Even if no one sees you do it – like getting sideways in a corner and just managing to keep it on the track – your heart pumps a bit, you get an adrenaline rush, and when you get back to the pits you've got that grin and you say to yourself 'Wow! That was cool.'

race was screwed for both of us. Our versions of what happened were different, but he's clear in his mind about it and so am I. As long as it doesn't happen again it can be called just a racing incident.

There was no time to be angry about what happened, because playing catch-up for the rest of the afternoon would require complete concentration. After an agonizingly slow trip back to the pits the team quickly replaced the tyre and back on the track the car felt really strong again. It would have to be because by this time we were in last place, nearly a lap behind the leaders.

Making up for the lost time meant having to push as hard as possible, while taking care to conserve fuel and tyres between pit stops and not overly stress the components of the car so we could get back into a point-scoring position. By lapping very quickly, sometimes quicker than the frontrunners, it was very satisfying to get up to sixth place. With Damon leading the race we would at least be able to contribute another point to the team's total, providing we made it to the finish. Unfortunately, this was not to be. With only five laps to go something broke at the rear end of the car and my San Marino Grand Prix was over.

It was just one of those days. You have to be philosophical about it. It was satisfying to make up all the lost time and get back into contention. The comeback was also productive from the point of view of having to revise strategy and adapt to the new circumstances, something that might be helpful another time.

TESTING TIMES

After the San Marino Grand Prix we stayed at Imola for a test session. It was tough, pounding around the same circuit after a hectic race weekend, and testing can be trying at the best of times. On a typical test day you get up at 7:00 and leave the hotel to get to the track by 8:00 to have breakfast and get ready to start driving at 9:00. Sometimes you drive a race distance or more, sometimes you stop every few laps to change something or talk to the engineers. If they make a big change to the car it can take a couple of hours and you stand around waiting. Then you stop for lunch which you have to eat and digest quickly because you're soon back on the track again, driving until 6:00 at night. Then you talk to the engineers some more and get back to the hotel about 8:00. You have a quick meal and then go into your room. Sometimes I listen to music or read a book for half an hour, and then crash into bed because in another few hours it will start all over again.

When you are testing, the feedback you give to the engineers is very important because they depend on you for the information they need to make changes to the car. I don't use technical terms when we talk. As a driver you have ideas of why the car behaves in a certain way, but you don't really discuss the technicalities with the engineer. It's not my job to know all the numbers and settings, so you talk about how the car is doing, how it feels and responds when changes are made.

I'm interested in all the technical stuff, but you can't clutter your mind with too much of it. In testing you're there to drive, to be on the edge out on the track, not at 95 percent but at nearly 100 percent. You can't go completely flat out all the time because you have to save a place in your brain to think about the car's reactions. But you have to be going quickly, otherwise you don't get the full picture. Then you come in and make the engineer understand what you feel and what you want.

One thing you learn when racing on an IndyCar oval track is to be patient and to study where the limit is. You cannot be right on the limit, where you might hit the wall, so you really have to learn to stay close to the limit without going over it. On high-speed ovals, particularly, you learn to become more sensitive to the feel of the car because at high speed even the slightest changes make a difference, much more so than on slower tracks. So this is a good experience to have, especially for setting up the car.

I prefer a car that handles predictably and suspension that is more hard than soft, which I hate because it's harder to drive to the limit. The goal is to arrive at a fairly even balance between the front and back, but if there is a choice between oversteer and understeer I like to have the rear end slightly looser, but not to the point of oversteering all the time. I am able to be more precise when the rear is lighter than the front. A snappy rear end can put you sideways more easily. You're not as far away from the edge but you can push that edge further, which is even more enjoyable.

MONACO GRAND PRIX

MONTE CARLO, MONACO, 19 MAY 1996

I have lived in Monaco for 17 years and was really looking forward to racing a Formula 1 car on my doorstep. But it all looked very different during the Grand Prix and it didn't feel much like home. So many people crammed into such a small space can cause problems, including the one which put me out of the race. At least I didn't have far to go when it was over.

T here was little time to relax and prepare for this important weekend. After the San Marino Grand Prix we stayed on at the Imola circuit for a busy test session, which was tough coming so soon after the race. A trip to Ireland for some public relations work and various other demands on our time meant there were only a few days at home, where it soon became even more hectic.

Racing here twice before in Formula 3 was of little use for the realities of Formula 1. The track was enjoyable in Formula 3, but I can't say it was much fun in my Williams Renault, especially in the beginning when I was trying to adapt to the differences. It was a totally new experience on what seemed a completely different track that had to be learned as if from scratch.

Because of the much wider car, those few sections of the very twisty track that used to be reasonably straight in Formula 3 become corners in Formula 1. The much higher Formula 1 speeds mean you are nearly always turning into all those corners, which requires much more braking, and this is made more difficult because hardly any of the braking areas are on a straight section.

Every lap required constant gear-changing, braking and accelerating, as well as perfect precision to keep the car away from the guard rails. The quicker corners, my favourites, were easier to learn, but the slower ones, a couple of them taken at less than 50 kilometres, were harder to get right.

On the first day of practice you are only allowed a total of 30 laps. I had found this was barely enough to get to know other tracks, and in Monaco it was not enough. I was losing time in the slower corners. I've always enjoyed quick corners, the faster the better. In skiing I much prefer downhill, as opposed to slalom, because you can get more of a high-speed rhythm going. In a racing car I am able to learn fast corners quickly, but usually need extra time to get up to speed in slow corners.

In qualifying, the combination of my not yet driving up to par and our losing the way somewhat with the car setup put us back in tenth place on the grid, by far the worst starting position to date. In the race-day warm-up session the two different setups we tried were inconclusive. But just before the race, in the short practice session in the rain, we were much quicker. The track was very slippery, but the conditions seemed to minimize our deficiencies. And since overtaking, notoriously difficult here, would be easier in the wet than in the dry I was actually hoping for a wet Monaco Grand Prix.

Just before the start it stopped raining, but the track was still treacherously wet and there were a lot of accidents. I drove as quickly and as carefully as possible, remembering the advice of Frank Williams and others in the team. They said Monaco is a race where if you finish, you finish well. But when you are

RELATIVE SPEED

Speed doesn't interest me in itself. In an airplane you can be going 500 miles an hour and you don't know it. But taking calculated risks while pushing the limit, knowing if you go over it you might crash, is where the pleasure is. And, despite its relatively slow speeds, there are plenty of places to crash in Monaco.

presented with an opportunity for overtaking you have to take advantage of it.

Before long we were running in the points, among a group of several closely matched cars. When the track became dry enough for racing slicks everyone stopped to change tyres and to take on fuel. Because the pit stops came earlier than expected, fuel conservation became a factor and my engineer Jock Clear came on the radio and told me to save fuel. Even so, there was a good chance of improving on our fourth place by the finish, providing we made it there.

The incident that put me out of the race happened when we were overtaking the slower Forti driven by Luca Badoer. After moving over to let the car in front of me go by he then cut across in front of me and we collided. Of course Badoer didn't see me. You never do such a thing on purpose. But once he moved over to let one car past he should have stayed there, because quite likely another car would be following closely behind. This was the view of the race stewards who later penalized Badoer for dangerous driving.

These things happen in racing, but it was very annoying to have my race ended by somebody else's mistake. As I sat on a kerb beside the track I must admit I felt more like going home than back to the pits. There was some consolation in meeting up with other drivers who had also been involved in accidents, and together we waited for the race to end. There were a lot of us (only three cars were still running at the finish), but there were no hard feelings and nobody wanted to talk about their problems.

You can't afford to dwell on the negative side of racing, and though we didn't score any points at Monaco there were some positive aspects to give us encouragement. There was some satisfaction in becoming much more competitive in the race after starting off badly. Though it also ended badly, the effort of finding out where I was going wrong and working hard to fix it was not wasted from the point of view of learning and improving. And even though it was a pointless weekend for Williams Renault – Damon led much of the way but had to stop because of a mechanical problem – we were still first and second in the drivers' standings and our team was still well ahead of the others.

And it was still the Monaco Grand Prix, with historic traditions to be observed. That evening Sandrine and I got together with some friends and went out for dinner and had a good party afterwards. We ended up with a group of about 14, including Mika Salo, who drives for Tyrrell now and is a good friend from the days when we raced in Japanese Formula 3, and David Coulthard, who drives for McLaren and also lives in Monaco. It was late at night and everybody was having fun.

SPEEDING IN MONACO

Apart from the slow corners, it's fun to drive a Formula 1 car through the streets of Monaco. But it's quite hard work – even for a Monegasque. The track never goes very far in any one direction, so you're always turning, you're on the brakes as much as you're on the acclerator, and you change gear about three dozen times on every lap.

On a flying lap the pit straight is not really straight, because you're actually turning to the right all the way into Virage de Sainte Dévote. Just before you start braking the track gets very bumpy, so that the car dips down, then up, which is a weird sensation. You can't overtake here, because the track narrows going into the corner and it becomes a real bottleneck, especially on the first lap when there is a huge traffic jam.

The climb up the Montée du Beau Rivage is very steep, with a wiggle in the middle, and there is also a high speed kink before you get to the Virage Massenet. When you go over the sharp rise before Massenet the car gets really light as it drops down. Through Massenet several different lines are possible, and you're braking as you're turning left. The turn gets progressively tighter as you go in and it's blind all the way around. You never think about not seeing where you're going. If you have time to think, you're too slow.

"Jacques is experiencing a learning curve – having to deal with his lack of knowledge of the circuits and setting up the car, which is very complex."

FRANK WILLIAMS *(Team Owner)*

The Virage Casino is a very strange corner. You're turning right, but just before the entry you have to jink around the guard rails which jut out onto the ideal line, and at the braking point the track becomes slightly banked. It drops off steeply at the exit of the corner, and when you accelerate down the hill you come very close to the guard rail. I'm told my father used to hit it but I never have.

On the descent to the Virage Mirabeau, the road surface is not flat but has a high crown in the middle, which makes it tricky for the heavy braking into Mirabeau. You can go into this right-hander fairly quickly, sometimes with your inside front wheel off the ground, because it is slightly banked to the outside which holds the car. Like every other corner here it's tight but still wide enough to overtake, providing you get the co-operation of the driver you're passing. I didn't in the race and this is where my Grand Prix ended.

Assuming you get around Mirabeau safely you then enter the stupid part of the track. The Virage du Loews is very slow – from 40 to 45kph – and a fairly useless corner. The kerb on the inside is quite high and you can climb it with the left front wheel. If you make a mistake and hit it with the back wheel, as I did once in the race, the car is launched into the air.

You accelerate downhill for a few metres to the next corner, a right-hander, which has another high kerb that you can put most of the right side of the car on. When you come off the kerb you're really bouncing, but you want to carry as much speed as possible into the Virage du Poitier.

You hit the brakes just before Poitier, a very important corner to get right because following it is the tunnel, and the quickest part of the track. You accelerate all the way through the tunnel, while turning gradually right, but it's easy to take flat out and not really very challenging.

Beyond the exit of the tunnel you're travelling faster than anywhere else on the track, and you have to brake very hard for the Nouvelle Chicane. You hit the brakes just where the track drops down a bit and you are also turning into the Chicane. The car gets really light and slightly airborne, another strange feeling, and then in the Chicane you have to avoid hitting the kerb. You're quite busy through here, but it's very slow and not much fun.

Then you come to the best part of the track: the section through the Virage du Tabac and La Piscine – the swimming pool. It's very bumpy in the braking zone for Tabac, where you go over some manhole covers, and then you're accelerating and turning left toward the first corner around the swimming pool. This is also a great corner, where you either brake or lift off slightly as you go in, and you have to judge your speed perfectly. The second corner, a right-hander around the pool, is not as difficult and you can drift out onto the kerb and use it as part of the track.

Accelerating through the next section, a gradual left-hander, is tricky because you lose adhesion on the road markings, including a pedestrian crossing, that are painted on the asphalt. Under braking for Rascasse you can slide on these even in the dry – it was much worse in the rain – and people were losing it here all weekend.

The Virage du Rascasse is another dead slow and boring hairpin, and as you accelerate out of it the traction is bad – more paint marks and a high crown in the road – and it feels like you're going nowhere.

The next corner, Virage Anthony Noghes, is another weird one. The guard rails crowd into the racing line so that you have five metres less road width than you really need, and there are more paint marks and a high crown. It's difficult to get it right, but you have to make a good entrance and exit here because, if you've not crashed, you're on the pit straight again and you've completed one lap of Monaco. Next year I plan to complete all the laps in the Grand Prix.

SPANISH GRAND PRIX

BARCELONA, SPAIN, 2 JUNE 1996

It was great to be on the podium at the end of a very wet and difficult Spanish Grand Prix. This race proved that experience is the best teacher, because unlike my first F1 race in the rain, in Brazil, I managed to go the distance without making a mistake. It was an achievement to even finish, on a day when so many cars didn't, and to be third behind the wet weather experts Schumacher and Alesi was quite satisfying.

On the six-hour journey by car from home in Monaco to Barcelona, it was encouraging to know our destination was a proper road course with lots of space where you could do some real racing. This would be welcome after the claustrophobic experience of the streets in Monaco. Not finishing that race meant it was important to get a good result and on the enjoyable Barcelona track, where we had a test day before the season began, the job would be easier. It's a lot of fun to drive, with a few high-speed corners, a long straight where you have a chance to outbrake people into the following corner, and some changes in elevation which add to the interest.

The previous knowledge of the circuit helped make it possible to be on the pace quickly, and the car felt really strong. In practice before qualifying on Saturday, just after we set the quickest lap of the session, a rare engine failure in our Williams Renault meant we were unable to perfect a qualifying setup. But we were still confident about our speed (I was even fined for exceeding the speed limit in the pit lane! – I was talking on the radio at the time and forgot about it), and this was proved with second place on the starting grid. It had been a good battle for pole position with Damon, and it was promising for the team to have the two of us on the front row. And then it rained on race day.

In fact, it poured – wiping out any advantage we had earlier in the weekend and forcing us, like everyone else, to experiment with wet weather setups in the 30-minute warm-up session. Before we got a chance to try what we thought might be a reasonable setup, the session was stopped because of an accident and we had to rely on guesswork to make changes to the chassis. With the rain coming down so heavily it also meant there would be a lot of guesswork for the drivers in the race – because of the poor visibility – except for whoever got in front at the start.

I managed to do this and on the run down to the first corner I was a bit surprised to be alone – though I enjoyed the solitude! All I could see in my mirrors was a torrent of water, like the wake from a boat, and for the rest of the afternoon many people went sailing. There were a lot of accidents and several times I felt on the verge of one. The car was twitching on nearly every corner of every lap. It was very treacherous and really easy to get caught out. You had to be extremely alert, and even then there was some luck involved in staying on the road. Every movement had to be smooth and delicate – never abrupt – but you couldn't slow down either.

It was impressive to see how quickly Michael Schumacher was able to go in such awful conditions. He was driving exceptionally well, and before long his Ferrari was in my mirrors. When he outbraked me going into a corner it was my turn to experience the very poor visibility in the spray. In places there were also rivers of water running over the track, and as if that wasn't enough, there was even some freezing rain falling at one stage.

It was miserable and cold in the cockpit, and with Jean Alesi now on my tail the situation was similar to Brazil, where I spun off when he tried to overtake me. I was determined that wasn't going to happen again, and it didn't, though he managed to get ahead during the shuffle of the running order after the pit stops. My car performed much better on the second set of rain tyres, and towards the end of the race I pushed really hard to catch Jean. It was a bit risky but I got close enough to keep him honest.

It was a tense and tiring race, fighting the track and the other cars for nearly two hours in the rain and cold. On the podium our teeth were chattering, but it felt great to be there. Since Damon didn't finish it was good to have scored points for the team. With Michael and me now tied in the standings, not far behind Damon, the championship was becoming more interesting and the next race, in Canada, would be exciting.

It certainly would be for me, racing in front of my home crowd. I didn't really know what to expect, other than a very hectic weekend. It would be nice to be able to perform up to the expectations of the Canadian fans. Their presence would be inspiring, but it wouldn't be possible to do more than I've done so far, which was to give my best all the time.

RACING IN THE RAIN

For someone with no previous experience of racing an F1 car in the rain, this season had so far provided plenty of learning opportunities. The weather in Spain was the worst yet, with really heavy rain from start to finish. It would be wrong to say I was now a wet weather expert, but on a day when only six cars were still on the track at the end of the 65 laps I had at least mastered some survival techniques. In wet conditions the racing line is usually better away from the dry line, because there is more adhesion on those parts of the track where no rubber has been laid down by the cars during dry conditions. The rain tyres, with their grooved tread pattern, bite down through the water (throwing it up into the faces of following drivers!) and grip the track. How successful the tyres are at doing this depends on the nature of the track surface, and this can vary a lot. Imola, for instance, where the asphalt is very smooth and the drainage not so good, would be undriveable at the speeds we were travelling at on the Barcelona circuit.

At least in Spain it stayed wet throughout the race, unlike in Brazil and Monaco where the track eventually dried out. The worst situation is the in-between stage, when there is both a wet line and a dry line and some cars have changed from wet to dry tyres. If you are on dry tyres and the car in front is still on wets, you can't use the wet line to overtake and often you get stuck behind it. The problem is worse on narrow circuits, like Monaco, where after my pit stop to change to dry tyres I came out behind a car that was still on wets, and before overtaking was possible I lost five seconds in one lap.

When a driver says he likes racing in the rain it usually means his car has a good wet weather setup. It's amazing how much grip an F1 car has in the wet. Maybe it has too much. The downforce works extremely well – but only when you are going fast enough to make it work. This means that you have to keep your speed up all the time, even on the straights, or you risk aquaplaning and losing control.

A wet track also heightens the imbalance in downforce between high- and low-speed corners. There is a big difference between the mechanical grip, the amount of adhesion inherent in the chassis and tyres, and the downforce grip, where the added pressure of air on the wings helps make the car stick to the track. With more downforce your car can be perfect for quick corners, but on tight corners, where you rely more on mechanical grip, the car won't stick nearly as well. Similarly, a car set up for slow corners won't work as well on faster ones, so that setting up the car is always a compromise in the wet, though more downforce is better.

When racing in the rain, the emphasis on downforce means you have to keep your foot down even though you can't always see where you're going. This heightens the dangers in poor visibility. When there is some distance to the car in front you can see the twin tracks left by its tyres. But when you close up on the car ahead the spray it leaves behind can be like hitting a wall of dense fog. It's even worse when the cars are bunched together, because the mist and water hangs in the air. The visibility problem is especially acute on the straights because you have no idea how fast the car in front is going. You're flat out on the throttle and you won't see the guy ahead until you're right on his gearbox. The red lights on the back of the cars are some help, but it's always hard to judge speeds. The car in front might even be stopped and you wouldn't know it until it was too late.

So there is always a certain amount of apprehension driving in the rain. You are under more stress and you feel the tension in your back and neck. You have to concentrate on staying relaxed because if you become too tense you don't drive as well. In the cockpit you try to do everything as smoothly as you possibly can, being especially gentle on the throttle and the brakes. The gear changing is all done automatically, so you can keep your foot down, though in really heavy rain you use short shifts to keep up the momentum while not disturbing the traction.

There are several reasons why some drivers are better than others in the wet. They may simply be smoother, or maybe they can adapt more quickly to finding the right lines and to recovering from getting sideways. Being able to quickly recover your car from moments of lost adhesion is a big advantage. A lot of this has to do with feel and experimentation. When you suddenly get sideways you can't tighten up and over-react, nor can you afford to slow down. You always have to keep pushing to the limits of the conditions, while staying within your own capabilities.

"When you have exceptional weather you have an exceptional result. Schumacher was brilliant and nobody could do anything to stop him. Despite the fact that Jacques is still not really used to the rain, he did well without making any mistakes."

BERNARD DUDOT
(Renault Sport Technical Director)

Car control on a wet track is mainly a question of feeling how close you are to the limit, and having the confidence to stay there. You need quick reflexes and fast reaction times and you also have to use your head. Staying on the road requires alertness, anticipation, a certain amount of informed guesswork and also some experimentation. To find out where to lift off in a corner you keep pushing until you start to slide, and then you back off, though there is no guarantee the conditions will be exactly the same on the next lap, so you have to be flexible in your thinking. It helps if you have a realistic imagination so that you can see in your mind's eye the various options available, and then think fast to choose the right one.

You have to be able to visualize the situation internally and understand where you are at any given moment in relation to the limits of adhesion.

Concentration is a vital part of racing in the rain, and in Spain I had to overcome physical distractions which threatened to make my attention waver. It was so wet and cold that I was shivering all afternoon. The cockpit provided little shelter – it felt like being on a motorbike in the winter – and then water started pouring into my helmet. This made the lack of visibility even more dangerous, because it happened when I was following other cars closely. In the vacuum created by the car in front the rain was sucked up under my helmet. When I passed the car the rush of air blew the water out of the vent of my helmet. I suppose this was a good incentive to keep overtaking people, and my other problem may also have increased my speed.

Before every race you have to drink a lot of water to prevent dehydration through the loss of body fluids from sweating. But it was so cold at Barcelona that there was not much sweating and the body fluids built up – most of them, it seemed, in my bladder! Maybe, because there was so much water around, the problem was made worse by the power of suggestion. The discomfort increased as the race went on, especially when I hit the brakes or shifted gears, and it was certainly a huge relief to see the chequered flag.

CHAPTER NINE

CANADIAN GRAND PRIX

MONTREAL, CANADA, 16 JUNE 1996

As expected, my home Grand Prix was a mixture of pressure and pleasure, both on and off the track. It was great to be back in Montreal, one of my favourite places, and to see all the interest in the race. But the expectations of the fans and the attention from the media created extra pressure to do well on the circuit named after my father. In the end, though a win would have been even better, second place after a good fight made me quite happy and the Canadian fans seemed to enjoy themselves as well.

It seemed a long time, longer than two weeks, since the last Grand Prix, but it was time well spent. Following a productive test session in Spain, we started our North American trip with an enjoyable visit to an IndyCar race in Detroit. My race engineer Jock Clear and several of the guys from our Williams Renault team came as my guests. I wanted them to see where I had raced for two years, and it was a good experience for all of us, made even more special because we were well looked after by my former IndyCar boss Barry Green and everyone at Team Green.

It was great to be at a race and not have to work, and it was fun to renew old acquaintances. I had forgotten how relaxed the IndyCar environment is, off the track at least, and by the time we left for Montreal we were well rested. We needed to be, because the whole week of my home Grand Prix was extremely hectic.

There was a lot of work to be done in Montreal, but at least it was in the familiar surroundings of a great city where I feel very comfortable. It's also the place where my girlfriend Sandrine attends university, and having her support during the pressure-packed days that followed was a bonus.

After all the pre-race activities it was a relief to get in the car on Friday, and to find that the circuit had been changed for the better and that our car was well suited to it. The removal of a slow chicane created a longer straight which provided more overtaking opportunities, and despite the lack of high-speed corners, where our superior aerodynamics are an advantage, our car was working very well. From the beginning we were right on the pace.

My previous experience here, winning a Formula Atlantic

race in 1993, was only useful in knowing where to turn left or right. The much higher cornering speeds and better braking power of an F1 car make it completely different from a driving point of view. But all that was second nature to me now, and as we became more experienced we were able to get everything together more quickly each weekend.

Right from the first day the track was packed with spectators, and by the end of the weekend an attendance record had been set. Obviously, since both my father and I were born a few kilometres away from here, most of the fans were cheering for me. But their enthusiasm was inspirational for all the drivers, and I don't think that performing in front of your home crowd should make you any faster. If you are quicker in your home Grand Prix it means you aren't working hard enough in the others.

It was impressive to see so many people enjoying themselves, and I was pleased to see that they were good sports. On Saturday, when Damon managed to beat me to get pole position, they even applauded him. The fans appreciated the show we put on in qualifying – it was a close fight with Damon just two hundredths of a second faster – and the race

NO SURPRISE

Some of the things that have happened to me certainly don't happen to everybody. I've been lucky and it's been great. But when you've done what you wanted to do, after working hard, and were expecting to do it, it doesn't seem so surprising.

turned out to be a battle between the two of us.

We decided to go with only one pit stop, while Damon chose to make two. Our strategy meant we started with a heavier load of fuel, so it was important for us to try and take the lead to prevent Damon taking advantage of his lighter car in the opening laps. Though our start went really well Damon's was equally good, and the difference between us, his pole position, was just enough for him to stay in front going into the first turn.

" It was a tough race right from the word go, you had to go flat out every lap. It was always going to be close with Jacques because there had never been more than a cigarette paper's width between us all weekend."

DAMON HILL *(Williams Renault Driver)*

That's the way we ran for the rest of the race, but it was not as straightforward as it sounds. I kept pushing him as hard as possible, so he would have to push as well and maybe make a mistake or run into trouble with backmarkers, and we were lapping almost as fast as in qualifying. The fans loved it, and near the end, when my car was lighter and I was able to get closer to Damon and set the fastest lap of the race, I could see the crowd waving and cheering more than ever. They must have been exhausted! It had all been great fun, and it was very satisfying to be able to reward their support with an aggressive drive and a strong finish.

It wasn't as good as winning, but it had been a hard and

satisfying race that produced a great result for the team. All of us worked really hard all weekend, and it paid off. My car was the best it had been so far, and the season was only half over.

CANADIAN DIARY

Monday...
12.00h. We arrived at Montreal airport. When I fly to Canada and the wheels of the plane touch down on the runway I always feel happy. I suppose it's something to do with returning to my roots.

13.00h. We checked into a downtown hotel where my girlfriend Sandrine was waiting. Her school is just around the corner. My manager Craig Pollock was staying in an adjoining suite and because we would be staying for the week we could actually unpack our suitcases.

19.30h. – Sandrine and I met some friends for dinner in a nearby restaurant. The friends treated me the same as always, which is why we're still friends. (One of them I've known since I was eight years old.) The only thing different are the changes in us from growing up, not our attitudes to each other. Things were different out on the streets. It seemed everywhere you looked there were billboards or posters and lifesize cardboard cutouts of me. It was somewhat unsettling to see a likeness of yourself staring back at you with a silly grin.

Tuesday...
We slept late and stayed in the hotel until the afternoon, when

we went shopping. By dressing casually and keeping my head low we managed to avoid crowds of racing fans. People would stare but weren't sure who they were seeing. I guess I didn't look like the guy wearing the racing suit in the cardboard cutouts – which were everywhere and becoming quite annoying. But the fans who recognized us were very polite and considerate – like good Canadians.

In the shops Sandrine concentrated on clothes, while I looked for books and CDs. I was interested in the latest Canadian bands and Quebec music, and also some of the more mainstream North American stuff which takes a while to get to Monaco. I bought quite a few CDs and stocked up on science fiction books, including some fantasy with humour, which is my latest interest. I buy for the future because I now have about 60 books waiting to be read.

Wednesday...
07.30h. A breakfast meeting in our hotel room to go over the plans for the rest of the week. There were a lot of demands being made, and I began to have thoughts of a mouse in a cage running on one of those treadmills.

11.00–14.00h. – A press conference in the Montreal Museum of Fine Arts, sitting under the glare of spotlights in front of about 250 mostly Canadian journalists and photographers. Then there were 15 separate radio interviews and 15 more for television. The idea was to get the media obligations over with in one session so we could then concentrate on racing. It was hard work, being the focus of attention in what was now being called 'Jackomania.'

The press conference was conducted bilingually. I found it funny when I thought about it later that with the French-speaking media I was speaking like a Québécois, which is different from the French that is spoken in France. Normally I do this if I'm speaking directly to a single person, but here I was doing it to a large group. I've always been able to switch from French to a Quebec accent without thinking. And it's the same between French and English. Sometimes with certain subjects it's easier to express myself in English, and when I'm speaking Italian I think in Italian.

No matter what the language, many of the questions in Montreal were about my father. This was certainly nothing new, and it was natural there should be more of them here since my home Grand Prix was at Le Circuit Gilles Villeneuve, where my father won his first F1 race (in 1978) and this year's race would be held on Father's Day. But what I found difficult was the inability of some people to accept the way I think. They see me as the son who should make the Villeneuve legend come alive again, and when I say we're two completely different people and that I'm my own person, they think it is a negative thing and that I have little regard for my father. This is pure stupidity because I love him dearly.

19.30h. The Williams team and some of our sponsors were my guests for dinner at a restaurant. There were about 75 of us and the dress code was 'Jacques-style' – very informal. We are friends and we work together, it was supposed to be a cool and relaxing evening, so why not dress in a relaxed way? It makes it easier to communicate when everyone is dressed casually. The evening was great fun and enjoyable for us all.

Thursday...
After sleeping in rather late, Sandrine and I went out with some friends to play computer games at an arcade. The computers were linked together and interactive and we had a great competition.

15.00–18.30h. We went out to the circuit to meet with the team and to talk to Jock Clear and the guys who work on my car.

19.00–20.00h. Damon and I attended a sponsor's event at the Verdun Auditorium where we were interviewed in front of a large crowd.

20.30h. Sandrine and I invited some friends to have dinner in our hotel suite. While we were waiting for room service, I went out to a shop and met a bunch of people on the street. Because I was alone they invited me to go to dinner with them. I found it amusing but it was another example of the kind of family atmosphere among the fans in Montreal.

Friday...
08.00h. We left to drive out to the circuit to go to work. Near the track the road was wet and muddy and someone bet me I couldn't put mud on the roof of the car. I drove through all the puddles but didn't manage to do it.

At the circuit I was amazed at the number of spectators – over 54,000 of them – and they all seemed to be waving flags, both the Canadian Maple Leaf and the Quebec Fleur de Lis. I'm not a political person so I always say I'm a Quebecer from

Canada. If you go to Mars then you're an Earthling. It was heartwarming to see how lively and happy the crowd was.

11.00–12.00h. It was a relief to finally get in the car. We set the fifth fastest time.

13.00–14.00h. We set the eighth fastest time, running with more fuel in the tank and concentrating on race setup. I felt confident for the race and thought a win was possible.

18.00h. We left the circuit earlier than usual, because the car was working well, and came back for another room service meal in the hotel. Craig joined us around the big marble table, and we talked about everything but racing which helped make it more relaxing. There was a lot of pressure in public, but in private I was very happy with the way things were going.

Saturday...
07.00h. We left the hotel and drove to the circuit for breakfast with the team. The crowd was bigger than ever – over 72,000 – and we were determined to give them something to cheer about.

09.00–09.45h. and **10.15–11.00h.** We set the fastest time in the combined practice sessions. The car felt really good and I thought pole was possible in qualifying.

13.00–14.00h. Damon beat me for pole by just two one hundredths of a second. It was very disappointing because I was sure that the car was quicker than my best lap time. The crowd didn't seem to mind, because it had been an entertaining battle, and they even cheered Damon.

16.35h. We left the circuit and returned to the hotel where I had a shower and then a massage from Erwin Gollner, the team physiotherapist. My sister Melanie arrived, from New York where she is studying music. It was great to see her again because we hadn't had a rendezvous for a while. She would watch the race with 15 others who were to be my guests in a suite above the pits.

Sunday...
06.45h. An early start for the big day. I'm not an early riser so it was difficult to get going, but we had to allow time for the traffic jams going into the circuit. Sandrine slept in because she would come later by helicopter. This was good for her because she's even less of an early riser than I am.

08.30–09.00h. Damon and I were first and second in the warm-up and we were looking good for the race.

09.30–12.30h. We talked to the team and chatted with our friends, then had a massage from Erwin and a light lunch in the Williams hospitality area.

13.00–14.36h. I chased Damon throughout the Grand Prix of Canada and finished 4.183 seconds behind him. The largest crowd ever to attend a single-day sporting event in Canada – over 100,000 people – watched us. I was sorry not to have won for them, but setting the fastest race lap and finishing second in my home race was the next best thing.

17.30h. We left the circuit and returned to the hotel to get ready for a big evening. Sandrine organised a dinner and party for about 40 of us at a restaurant owned by a friend of ours. Usually, a post-race event like this is a formal gala with sponsors, and you have to dress up and speak to a lot of people you don't know. But this was just a party Sandrine had put on for me, with cool people, including Mika Salo and David Coulthard, who are two guys you can have fun with.

After dinner we went to a disco, where some of the Williams mechanics joined us, and then about 15 of us went back to the restaurant where we had a floor to ourselves. Sandrine brought a sound system and our own music, and the party lasted until 6 in the morning. Often you go out after a race and have a few drinks, then you get bored. But this was great fun. There were a lot of people to talk to, and not about racing. We had a blast and that happens so rarely. It had probably been years since I attended a party like that. It was a good way to finish the weekend, and the first half of my first F1 season.

Monday and Tuesday...
We weren't leaving until Wednesday, so there were a couple of days to rest and enjoy Montreal. Once the race was over it was as if everyone went back to their normal lives. People seemed not to recognize me as much, and if they did it was after I had gone by. We were all just minding our own business, which is the way I like it.

I took some time to go and see my grandmother and catch up on all the family news. We visited other friends, including one who is a singer and was making a recording at a studio. Another friend was getting married on the following Saturday, but unfortunately I wouldn't be able to attend. Sandrine represented us, while I flew back to Europe to go testing again – back to the racing life.

"I think his first half of the season has been fantastic. His first race was unbelievable. So I really think he has a great chance for the future."
JACKIE STEWART *(Three-time World Champion)*

" Damon Hill has a teammate in Jacques Villenueve who has been pushing him all the way, though probably not to the extent that he could next year with greater experience."
MICHAEL SCHUMACHER
(Ferrari driver and World Champion)

" Of course I think he is very quick. Look at his results!"
JEAN ALESI *(Benetton driver)*

Mid-term Report

The Canadian Grand Prix was the eighth of the 16 races, and at the halfway point in my first F1 season I was happy with the progress made. Looking back, it was satisfying to see almost continual improvement. The experience gained in the first three races led to the win at the Nürburgring, and even the occasional setback contributed to more positive results later on. For instance, the lessons learned from spinning out in the rain in Brazil were put to good use in the very wet Spanish Grand Prix.

Each weekend, though most of the circuits were new to me, we were on the pace earlier – partly because I was driving better, but also because our teamwork improved as we got to know each other better through racing and testing. I understood the car more and Jock Clear and the mechanics had a better idea of what I wanted. This made our jobs easier, because we wasted less time arriving at a good setup and could get down to business sooner. But we could still benefit from getting up to speed quicker, especially in qualifying where I was lagging a bit behind.

In qualifying for the first eight races we were on pole once, second on the grid three times, third three times and then tenth quickest at Monaco, which was my only really bad qualifying performance. The way to improve in qualifying would be to spend less time working on the race set up and work more in practice on Friday and Saturday with low fuel and new tyres to simulate qualifying conditions. Every second counts in qualifying – even fractions of a second as we found out in Canada, where two hundredths of a second behind Damon on the grid had a big influence on the race results.

" Speaking for myself, I'm delighted with Jacques. He is after all a rookie in F1, and to be second in the drivers' championship at the halfway stage says all I need to say."

FRANK WILLIAMS *(Team owner)*

I failed to finish three of the eight races and each of the retirements was due to an incident in the race. Last year in IndyCar racing I finished every race in which there wasn't a mechanical failure. So far in 1996 our Williams Renaults had proved wonderfully reliable, which made my non-finishes more annoying. I was very unhappy about making the mistake which put me out of the Brazilian Grand Prix. At least there was no one else to blame, unlike the other two retirements where other drivers were involved. In the San Marino Grand Prix, before we had to stop because of damage probably caused in the first lap collision, our speed showed we were well-placed to get a good result. At Monaco it was very frustrating to be put out of the race by another car, because it cost us some easy points that were there for the taking after all the main championship contenders also failed to finish.

Still, I made it to the podium in every race I finished. And from a results point of view – with one win, three second places and one third place in five races – the overall performance was quite respectable for a newcomer to F1. Yet I had the speed to win other races, and might have done so had the circumstances been only slightly different. We very nearly won in Australia, but had to slow down with an oil leak. A win in Canada was possible because we had the speed, but our second place on the grid (by two hundredths of a second) was a handicap. Even in the San Marino race, though we were out of the running after the first lap incident, we were also quick enough to win.

" He is clearly a very fast driver in overall racing car terms. Of that there is no doubt. But whether he is a very fast racing driver in comparison to the very best in Formula 1 – people like Ayrton Senna and Michael Schumacher – I don't think there is evidence to say that yet. "

JONATHAN PALMER
(BBC TV Commentator and former F1 driver)

In the drivers' standings my 32 points in the first half of the season left me in second place behind Damon, who had been more consistent in finishing at the front. But overall I had been able to achieve my goal, which was to be competitive and be able to challenge the frontrunners. That would still be the objective in the remaining races, where the experience gained in the first half of the season would be helpful in the competition which was bound to become even more intense.

" I think Villeneuve will give Damon Hill a hard time in the second half of the year."

KEN TYRRELL *(Team owner)*

" Clearly, anyone who can win a Grand Prix, the Indy 500 and the IndyCar championship is a great racing driver. There is no doubt that he is a world-class driver. It is difficult to rate him in absolute terms at the moment because he has had a car advantage. He really has not known the circuits that well. We will have to wait a little bit longer to make a final judgement."

MARTIN BRUNDLE *(Jordan driver)*

FRENCH GRAND PRIX

MAGNY-COURS, FRANCE, 30 JUNE 1996

Considering my big crash in qualifying and the pain in the neck it caused, second place was a good result in the French Grand Prix. With Damon winning the race we got the best possible result for the Williams Renault team.

After the pressures of my home Grand Prix in Canada, we had enjoyed a couple of relaxing days in Montreal before heading for Silverstone to test some things which Jock Clear and I wanted to try before the French race. This was an important event for our engine supplier Renault, and also special for me because I have lived in this part of the world for many years. I drove up from Monaco to Magny-Cours by car, and though it took six hours because there was a lot of traffic, we arrived refreshed and feeling optimistic about our chances.

My neck was actually sore before the race weekend started, possibly from air conditioning in the hotel. But that was soon forgotten when practice began on the Magny-Cours circuit. Getting up to speed quickly was made even easier by new and more powerful engines from Renault, and we were fairly confident about qualifying.But periodic rain during the Saturday morning practice session made it necessary to change the car setup frequently to suit the wet conditions. We only managed about five laps with a dry setup which, as it turned out, was needed for qualifying. Our time on the first set of tyres was reasonable, but my first lap on the second set of tyres was not as quick as expected so I set my mind to pushing really hard on the next lap.

Coming out of one of the faster corners on the circuit, at about 220 kilometres per hour, the car went a little bit wide but, not wanting to lose the lap, I chose not to lift off. The car went over a kerb, and for a moment the wheels were off the ground. When they touched down it was on wet grass, which made braking useless and steering nearly impossible. Any hope of regaining control was lost when a dip in the ground launched the car into the air just before it ploughed into a tyre barrier.

In this case the tyres in front of the concrete wall were a disadvantage, because the car was travelling nearly parallel to the wall and might have been able to slide along it to dissipate some of the energy. Instead, there was a big impact when the tyres grabbed the car, stopping it very suddenly (by this stage it was probably doing about 200 kilometres per hour), then throwing it back onto the track.

Another car nearly hit me before the red flag was shown to stop the session, but the damage was already done. The car was badly wrecked, and somehow my helmet had hit either the steering wheel or the windscreen and there were also paint marks on it from hitting the tyres. Still, it could have been worse.

" I was really surprised how well Jacques was able to race. His neck was in quite bad shape but it didn't seem to slow him down."

ERWIN GOLLNER
(Williams team physiotherapist)

Normally, it is thought drivers should take their hands off the wheel in these situations, but keeping my hands on the steering wheel had helped me in a couple of heavy crashes in IndyCar racing. All that force has to go somewhere, and if you don't deflect it by gripping the wheel a lot of it will be transferred into your shoulder straps, which could break a collarbone, or even your neck.

SECOND FIRST TIME OUT
After starting from pole and leading most of the way a mechanical problem cost the win in my first race, in Australia.

IN AT THE DEEP END
My first F1 race in the rain, in Brazil, was fun until I made a stupid mistake and spun out of second place into a gravel trap.

LEARNING FAST
New circuits, unfamiliar opposition, discovering how the car behaved in racing conditions – every race in 1996 was a learning experience.

MY FAVOURITE FAN
Sandrine is not really a race fan. But having her there provides a feeling of normality and helps take away some of the stress.

TEAM SUPPORT
Having the full support of owner Frank Williams and everyone on the team made it easier to get up to speed more quickly.

MONACO ON THE ROCKS
It helps to have an attractive part of the world to come home to. Monaco also has some good places for roller-blading on seaside paths.

STARTING FIRST
My fourth race, the European Grand Prix, began with a quick start and featured a race-long battle with the local hero, Michael Schumacher.

A TEAM OF WINNERS
Williams is a winning team with a winning car. Everything is there to win so all I have to do is my job, which is to try to win.

FINISHING FIRST
Victory in the European Grand Prix was a great feeling, made extra special because my first F1 win had come so soon.

STARTING TROUBLES (inset)
Being hit from behind at the start meant having to play catch-up in the San Marino Grand Prix.

COMEBACK SETBACK (main photo)
It was satisfying to fight back from last place and into contention but annoying to have to stop before the finish.

RENAULT POWER
Christian Contzen and Bernard Dudot and the people at Renault Sport make engines that are powerful, reliable – and waterproof.

THE BARCELONA CIRCUIT
The site of the Spanish Grand Prix is challenging and fun to drive – providing you can see where you're going.

THE RAIN IN SPAIN
With the severe visibility problems it was useful to be in front at the start. And finishing third was rewarding in such treacherous conditions.

ANATOMY OF AN ACCIDENT

This was my worst accident in F1, though I had several bigger ones in IndyCar racing. Looking back, I could have avoided it by lifting off, but I was prepared to take the risk because grid positions were especially important on the tight circuit which hasn't got many places to pass.

In qualifying we planned to do three runs of two laps each. My best lap on the second run wasn't quick enough. When I saw the lap time I was very determined to be more aggressive on the next lap, even though the car was not performing at its best because the wet track in the morning had prevented us from arriving at a proper dry setup.

On the first quick corner in the previous qualifying laps the car was understeering and had pushed wide to the outside of the asphalt, but the kerb helped keep it on the track and I didn't have to lift off. This time there was a bit more understeer but I thought the kerb would help again, so I kept my foot to the floor. I was really going for it. Just before hitting the kerb I knew I was running out of track, but usually you can put two wheels on the grass and keep going, maybe losing a tenth of a second or so. I didn't know the kerb sloped sharply on the other side and I also forgot the grass was still wet from the rain in the morning. Both these facts became obvious when it was too late to do anything.

When I went over the kerb I was still going flat out. The car bottomed out on the kerb, with the wheels off the ground, and then it hit the wet grass and started sliding losing hardly any speed. I started coming off the throttle to try and get back on the track, but by this time I was mainly just a passenger. Then the car hit a small dip in the grass and was launched into the air. It was bouncing when it landed, and about 20 metres later it stuffed itself into the tyre barrier.

In the few seconds before hitting the barrier I at first thought the angle of impact would be slight, and the car would just slide along it harmlessly. But when I saw the tyres looming up I thought: 'Shoot! This is going to be a big hit.' I gripped the steering wheel as hard as I could and pushed backwards to counter the force of the impact.

Holding on to the steering wheel in an accident is not supposed to be the thing to do, but I've always done it, to absorb the impact and prevent the upper body from being thrown forward as far. The argument against holding on is that you risk injury from the flailing wheel. It seems to me that before that happens the pressure you exert on the steering wheel would cause it to break off. Anyway, I'd rather break a wrist than my neck, and I've had some practical experience that put my theory to a heavy-duty test. In one big accident in IndyCars I actually bent the steering wheel. If the wheel hadn't absorbed the force it might have been a part of my body that bent or broke.

In France, as it turned out, I was lucky not to break anything but the car. When it hit the tyres it stopped dead, before rebounding back on to the track. In the shock of the impact it didn't register that my helmet had bounced off both the tyres in the barrier and the steering wheel or the windscreen of the car. I felt neither blow, nor did I see them, though my eyes were open all the time. All I remember is seeing the steering wheel a few centimetres in front of my face.

The accident didn't really happen in slow motion as you sometimes hear them described. Maybe I'm getting used to them! The first one I had, a few years ago, felt more like it was happening in slow motion, but this one was in real time and I was aware of everything. Before the car stopped spinning I had already spoken to the guys in the pits on the radio. They tell me I said: "******* Hell! That was a big one!"

I had wanted to let them know what was going on, but they already knew – so did the world! – because the in-car camera in my Williams was on the whole time. Most embarrassing. But it wasn't over yet. My wrecked car was parked in the middle of the track, and the next thing I saw was David Coulthard's

DANGEROUS THOUGHTS

I never think about the danger, but it's probably unhealthy to think you are immortal. I am fearful of things you don't have control over. In a car if you start getting sideways you have a chance to catch it. But if I was in an elevator and it started to fall I would probably be scared.

Though I've never been really frightened in a racing car, sometimes after a big moment or a crash you think for a few seconds 'Whew, that could have hurt.' But you're not hurt so you say it with a smile. And you feel stronger because you're not hurt. Maybe, because I've never hurt myself badly in a racing car, it never feels as though it could happen. In a way this allows you to go to the limit, because you want to be out on the edge and feel you can control it to get the biggest rush out of it.

McLaren flying by at terrific speed. I thought: 'Holy Macaroni! I'm lucky he didn't hit me!' Then they stopped the qualifying session, and I climbed out of the car and waved to the crowd to show I was okay.

During the accident there was no time to be afraid. There was time later, but I've never been fearful for myself, though I have been afraid for other people who might be involved in my accidents. So far, I've never hurt myself badly and this one only left me with a sore neck. It didn't slow me down and in the race it nearly happened again. A couple of times the car started to go over the same kerb but I solved the problem by lifting off – partly because I thought it would look really stupid to crash at the same spot!

After the accident the doctors said I was okay to get right back in the car. Personally, I don't think you should be allowed to drive immediately after having a big crash. You should take at least the rest of the day off, because no matter how fit you feel you are still likely to be suffering from some shock. Your adrenaline could be masking the pain from an injury and, in the heat of the moment, it is also possible for a driver to hide the truth so he can get back to racing. I'm sure there are cases when drivers have gone back out after an accident when they weren't really fit enough to do it. Their judgement might be impaired, and that can be dangerous for them and everyone else.

Because of my experience with accidents, I knew exactly what shape I was in and I also new my neck would get worse before it got better. After one IndyCar crash I had no problem at all until a day later, when my neck started to hurt. It got progressively worse and was sore for about a month. In that case I didn't have the benefit of a physiotherapist like Erwin Gollner.

Erwin really helped in France, massaging my neck to relieve the stiffness and soreness and applying his magic potions. After the race he drove back to Monaco with me and did some more of his good work there. On race weekends he also helps make sure we get the right nutrients in our food and drinks. I enjoy his company and we get along well. It's possible to relax with him so that even the strict regimes he forces on us don't seem like work.

Erwin only works on my body, not my mind. I think it's up to a driver to prepare himself psychologically. You should be able to look after your own mind. I also don't believe in pre-race rituals, like saying a prayer, wearing a certain colour of underwear or getting into your car the same way every time. I don't believe in such superstitions. I walk under ladders and don't care if a black cat walks in front of me.

I believe in what goes around comes around, but I don't believe in fate. It's too easy to blame problems on fate. If there is anybody to blame it should be yourself. The accident in France was completely my fault. One hundred percent.

BRITISH GRAND PRIX

SILVERSTONE, ENGLAND, 14 JULY 1996

My second F1 victory may not have been as dramatic as the earlier one at the Nürburgring, but winning at Silverstone was more important because it tightened up the championship battle with Damon. While it was good to be standing on the top step of the podium again, and also satisfying to win Damon's home race after he won mine in Canada, the results of the British Grand Prix reduced his lead in the standings to just 15 points.

The week before the race we had a successful test session at Silverstone and all of us, race engineer Jock Clear and the guys who work on my car, were feeling very optimistic about our prospects. Following the test there was just enough time for a couple of days back home in Monaco to work on my fitness. My neck was still a bit sore from the accident in France but after some heavy-duty training (including running in the hot sun on the paths beside the Mediterranean) I was in good shape physically, and feeling strong mentally.

Our optimism was boosted by the fact that for the first time this season we would be racing on a circuit I know well. Silverstone is the home circuit of our Williams Renault team, and all the testing we had done there would put me on a more equal footing. Though Damon knows the track even better, and he would also have the advantage of having his home crowd behind him, I was determined to take an aggressive approach to the whole weekend.

On Friday we were quickly on the pace and managed to set the fastest time of the day, even though the car didn't feel quite as good as it had in testing. Somehow there was less grip, but the speed was there and we were also fastest in the first half of the qualifying session on Saturday. Damon was in good form, as usual, and we had an exciting battle for pole position. Late in the session, after Damon had set a quicker time, my chance to respond was spoiled slightly by a slower car and I had to settle for second on the grid. A close second in qualifying might seem respectable, but it was a big let-down on a day when I was so determined to get pole.

To beat Damon a good start would be essential, but beyond

that we had to improve the race setup. The car was good for a quick lap in qualifying, though it still felt a bit too nervous for 61 laps of what we expected would be hard racing. In the warm-up on Sunday morning Jock Clear and I arrived at a setup that made the car feel very good with a load of fuel. We made plans to stop twice for fuel and tyres, and adopted a strategy for the start which was straightforward: take the lead and quickly open up as big a gap as possible.

That's exactly what happened, though we got some help from Damon. His start was as bad as ours was good, and several cars overtook him before the first corner. Meanwhile, Jean Alesi also got a great start and we were wheel-to-wheel for a few moments before he dropped back to second place. With the advantage of a clear track ahead, I was able to push hard and build up a cushion of over 20 seconds before the first pit stop. Shortly after that Damon's race ended, when a problem with a wheel caused him to spin off. I can't say I was unhappy to see him go, though I know it was disappointing for him and for the British fans.

With Damon out of contention it was important to finish and score points for the team, as well as for myself, but I couldn't afford to stop pushing. With some of the cars behind on a single pit stop strategy it was important to build up another cushion to accommodate our second stop. This was fairly easy to do because the car was working perfectly, and when it became time to stop again we had a lead of over half a minute.

In the remaining laps we opened up a comfortable gap, and all we had to do was stay alert and keep out of trouble until the finish. The main job was to avoid making any mistakes when lapping slower traffic. At this stage you also worry about the possibility of mechanical problems, but the car was as reliable as it was quick.

There was no close opposition and it may have been a bit boring to watch, but it certainly wasn't in the cockpit. It was hard work on a hot and humid afternoon, and Silverstone has some high g-force turns that become quite tiring over a full race distance. Near the end I was able to ease up a bit, and crossing the finish line with no one close behind meant I could savour the moment more.

"When Jacques missed getting pole in qualifying he was, privately, very angry with himself. The last time I saw him do this, before an IndyCar race, he drove even more aggressively than usual and won the race easily."

CRAIG POLLOCK *(Manager)*

It was a great feeling. It's always good to win, but this one felt especially good because it was overdue. After our first win, at the European Grand Prix in April, we had some good results, but most of the time it seemed we were second while Damon was doing the winning. There had been races I could have won and others where I should have scored more points. The win in Britain also showed how quickly things can change in the championship.

We had a big lead in the team standings and Damon and I would be free to fight each other for the championship. Our rivalry was friendly and confined to the track only, but we both relished the challenge. He would have an advantage at the next three races, in Germany, Hungary and Belgium, because I had never been to the circuits. But then I had never seen the Nürburgring before I won the race there.

CAR NUTS

At Silverstone, and before the start of each race, the drivers are paraded around the track in open cars so the spectators can get a closer look at us. As an added attraction for automotive enthusiasts we usually ride in famous old cars – but they don't mean much to me.

I've never been what you would call a car nut, the type of person who puts posters of classic vehicles on the wall, or spends hours going through car magazines, or uses their spare time to tinker with their cars. I do have some interest in the scientific and mechanical side of automobiles. In school I enjoyed math and physics and I like to know how things work, but there is no way I could repair a car properly. I might be able to get it running, but my knowledge is very basic. I used to work on my own motocross bike, and even when I was quite young I would try to fix my computer if it broke down. If it still didn't work I would bang it and sometimes that did the trick.

For personal transport I can't see the point of having a high performance 'jet-set' type of car. You don't need a car that does 350 kilometres per hour. Where can you use it? Anyway, even going 200 on a motorway is boring. I drive fairly quickly on public roads but don't push the limits. When you do it for a living you're less inclined to speed when you don't have to.

I love racing and I enjoy driving on public roads, but a car to me is mostly a means to an end. You race them to win and you drive them to get where you're going. I enjoy helping set up a racing car so it will be quicker, but I don't enjoy washing and polishing a road car. Any road car of mine is usually a mess inside, and if I get a dent in it, well too bad. I take much better care of my computer.

For me an F1 car is not necessarily a thing of beauty. The styling is a bit too extreme, and with the high noses and big wings they're looking less and less like basic racing cars, which have a kind of functional beauty. I can appreciate the eccentric styling in some older road cars, like the American cars from the 1960s, with all the chrome and the big fins. In modern cars the Dodge Viper is interesting because it is so outrageous, and a vehicle like the Mini Moke is great because it's so primitive.

To some people the sound of engines is like music. I love music but hate noise that hurts the ears. If you seldom hear them it must be impressive to listen to F1 engines, and you can imagine all the mechanical stuff that's going on inside them. But because I spend so much time sitting a few centimetres in front of a Renault V10 it's much less of a novelty.

In the F1 season we race 16 times and we're testing a great deal of the time between events. On top of that, if you need to listen to cars, to look at them and spend hours working on them and making them shine, then I think you've got a problem. There is more to life than that. If the only thing you enjoyed was cars then you would surely be a bore to your friends.

Despite my attitude to cars I am happy there are others who feel more strongly about them. Otherwise there might be fewer racing fans.

SETUP SEMINAR

A really good setup, which made the car handle so well, was an important factor in being able to win the British Grand Prix. In setting up the car the objective is to bring the handling to a point where you are comfortable with it, so that you can trust it and have the confidence to be able to push hard consistently.

While setting up the car depends heavily on many different technical factors, the input from the human side, especially from the driver, is also very important. It's not a robot driving the car, and though every driver does it differently, it's mostly done by feel.

To make your feelings known, and to have them translated into setup changes, you need a good relationship with your race engineer and the mechanics. They have to understand how you drive and what you want from the car. When you say to them that the car is performing in a certain way it's not something you will find in a textbook or a dictionary. The communication is something very personal – almost like a private code – that only becomes understood after you've been working together awhile. It takes time for the race engineer to understand what you mean and to interpret your feedback into practical solutions to setup problems.

It also takes time for the driver to learn to give the right feedback. It's not good enough just to say the car is getting sideways. There may be ten reasons for this, so you have to understand them and be able to explain it to your engineer. When the engineer knows you better he can interpret it more quickly and your experience of working together speeds up the process. Often we can look back at something in the setup that was used earlier and start working with that.

Mutual trust between the driver and engineer is also important. When you are trying something new on a car the engineer can say 'trust me on this' and you go out on the track and try as hard as you can. If you spin out at least you've tried, and you must still believe in your engineer, and he in you.

Jock Clear, my race engineer, checked me out early in our relationship. Coming from IndyCars I had definite ideas of what I wanted in a setup – ideas that were quite different to what Damon was using in the other Williams Renault. At one test, unknown to me, Jock did the opposite of the setup change I requested and sent me out on the track. When I came back in I told him I felt the difference, that the car was not doing what I expected it to do after my request. After checking me out in this way Jock trusted my feedback more.

I think the race engineer should also rely more on what the driver says, instead of relying completely on the computer data. This is not easy to do in F1 where computers are more established. It was easier in IndyCars where we used the computer mostly as backup to the driver's feedback. In F1 there is a tendency for the reverse to be true, to believe that the computer data is more often right than the driver and to rely on the computer for answers to setup questions. I love computers, but I also believe in my backside – the feedback from the driver – when it comes to setting up a racing car.

For the driver, the numbers and graphs provided by the computer are useful to see where you're getting the most out of a lap, where you're slower or faster on any given part of the circuit. To make the computer work for you it is vital to be able to understand what the numbers mean. This is where it is important for the driver, working with the engineer, to be able to put a physical face to the numbers. It is only when you know what the car is doing in relation to the numbers that the computer really becomes a useful setup tool.

The engine is the most difficult thing to feel and you rely more on the computer for that. In our team the Renault people do most of the engine setup work. As a driver what you want above all is good drivability – usable power over the widest range of conditions at each circuit. This means that torque – pulling power – is as important as horsepower. Because F1 engines rev very highly, and the usable range of power is limited, it is important to have the right gear ratios to make the best use of the power. In choosing gear ratios much depends on the configuration of the circuit, but you always end up making a compromise.

In fact, all setup work is a compromise because there are so many variables. How the car handles involves a mixture of hundreds of components (there are something like 10,000 parts in an F1 car) working together. Basically, the setup can be affected by adjustments to the front wing, the rear wing, the dampers, springs, suspension settings, camber, toe-in, tyre pressures, ride height, brake balance, weight transfers, the rake of the chassis, and so on. All these factors are interactive, and they can change constantly according to the car's fuel load, the condition of the tyres, the track conditions, the weather, and so on.

My ideal setup is to have a neutral-handling car. If it's not possible to achieve a completely neutral setup, then I prefer a tendency to oversteer. With oversteer, when the rear wheels slide out, you can always compensate. It's easier to spin off or crash and it's more tiring to drive, but you can push the limit more. I hate understeer, because when the front wheels don't turn as much as you need it sets a limit on what you can do in cornering and you have to back off.

Understeer can sometimes be dialled out of the chassis by increasing the front wing rake – to bring the centre of pressure forward – or by playing with the front anti-roll bar. Sometimes the front bar can be set too soft and the car becomes sluggish. Understeer can also be caused by the setup situation at the back of the car. It's all very complex and at different times you can have several cures for the same problem.

It's impossible to keep track of everything, though it helps when you've built up a store of knowledge so that you can remember how certain changes made the car behave in the past. But from the driver's point of view setup work is mainly a matter of transforming gut feeling into mechanical certainty.

GERMAN GRAND PRIX

HOCKENHEIM, GERMANY, 28 JULY 1996

Finishing third in the German Grand Prix was disappointing, but it was satisfying to race reasonably well after overcoming earlier problems. Also on the positive side was maintaining the record of making it to the podium in every race I had finished, which contributed to the big lead our team had in the Constructors' Championship. Less positive, from a personal point of view, was that by winning in Germany Damon extended his lead in the drivers' standings.

After winning the British Grand Prix it was great to be able to celebrate with a week off at home in Monaco. This was the first real holiday we had had since the European part of the season began and my girlfriend Sandrine, on a break from university in Canada, was able to enjoy it with me. It was very relaxing, though there was a lot of work to do around the flat, as well as some training to catch up on. Still, it was a welcome return to a more normal world, which is important to help a driver deal with the pressures of racing life.

The realities of racing soon returned when we went to a test session at the Paul Ricard circuit in France on the Monday before the race in Germany. The test, to experiment with the low downforce settings we would need on the long straights at Hockenheim, wasn't as productive as we had hoped, but we were still optimistic about our chances in Germany. The race would be crucial in our fight for the championship because the relatively straightforward Hockenheim circuit would be easier to learn, compared to the more complicated circuits in Hungary and Belgium, which would also be new to me.

I liked the Hockenheim layout, though I was surprised at how bumpy it was in some places, and the high speeds on the straights reminded me of some of the super speedways in IndyCar racing. Practice on Friday started out well enough, but after the first few laps we stopped making progress. The car became difficult to drive – it was very twitchy – and no matter what we tried in the way of changes to the setup we couldn't seem to cure a mysterious handling problem.

There was another setback on Saturday morning when our practice session was interrupted by an engine failure after only nine laps. When the car stopped out on the circuit I ran across the track to try and get back to the pits as quickly as possible, and the race stewards summoned me to appear before them for crossing the track illegally. That problem was solved when I explained that a marshal had given me permission to cross the track. But bigger problems remained. Besides the persistent handling difficulties we would have to qualify without having done many laps running with low fuel, and we would also have to use an older specification Renault engine on a track where power is of prime importance.

Considering our disadvantages, sixth place on the grid was reasonable after a very exciting hour of qualifying. Right near the end of the session, we were on a quick lap which might have been closer to Damon's pole time except for a slight mistake in the last part of the lap. As it was we were less than a second away from him, and all the cars on the first three rows of the grid were very evenly matched. A good start would be vital, and taking advantage of any overtaking opportunities would require top performance from car and driver.

But my car was still not performing as it should, and having an ill-handling car undermines a driver's confidence. It's easier to accept this kind of situation if you know what's wrong, and sometimes you can adjust your driving accordingly. But up to this point we were faced with a mystery we couldn't seem to solve. Our only hope was that a solution could somehow be found before the race, and we were delighted when that proved to be the case.

In the warm-up session on Sunday morning we discovered the problem. A shock absorber had been broken on the right side at the front of the car all weekend.

With a new shock absorber the car was transformed and,

luckily for us, we got a chance to try it before the start. During the drivers' parade a heavy shower soaked the circuit (and the drivers!) and we were given a special acclimatization session to come to grips with the wet track. As it turned out the race was dry, but in the 15-minute session we managed to set the quickest time. This was a great relief, but also annoying because the car was now where it should have been on Friday. The race was still going to be a matter of making up for lost time and it would be important not to let the earlier frustrations adversely affect my driving.

"Don't count Jacques out. I'm certainly not. He is still a serious challenger for the championship, and it is going to be very interesting for the remaining races."

DAMON HILL *(Williams driver)*

The start went smoothly, and in the early laps I was careful not to become overly aggressive and push the car too hard. We still weren't sure if we had chosen the right race setup, and our decision to make only one pit stop meant starting with a heavier load of fuel than some of the others, including Damon.

Gradually, it became clear that my car was capable of being driven hard, and with that realization came the confidence to make the best use of it.

While Damon and the two Benettons were fighting for the lead those of us in the following group were often very close together. These battles were quite stimulating, and the highlight of the race for me, though it probably wasn't for the

German fans, was overtaking Michael Schumacher's Ferrari.

We both made pit stops at the same time, and Michael was in front when we returned to the track. To pass him I thought it would be important to strike quickly, and maybe catch him by surprise. It worked. I don't think Michael was expecting me to make a move on him going into the first chicane, where he was a couple of car lengths ahead. I pulled out from behind, braked later than he did, and just managed to overtake him. From then on it was mainly a question of staying out of trouble and pressing on to the finish.

It's hard to say if more than third place would have been possible had we discovered the shock absorber problem earlier in the weekend. Anyway, you can't afford to dwell on what might have been. Instead, you have to look ahead. Damon was now 21 points ahead, with five races to go in the championship. It would be an uphill struggle, but so was the German Grand Prix.

PUBLIC SPEAKING

With all the media commitments on a Grand Prix weekend it sometimes seems as if we're talking more than driving. Besides having to talk to the F1 journalists there are usually appearances arranged by our sponsors to speak to their guests. Most of the press conferences and interviews are scheduled previously, but you also have to contend with impromptu situations.

As soon as you get out of the car at the end of each track session you're surrounded by journalists who want an up-to-the-minute account of your progress. Then you sometimes have a half-hour of regularly scheduled interviews, and often a team press conference. On Friday you can be selected for the Friday Five press conference. On Saturday if you qualify in the top three there is another press conference, and if you make it to the podium on Sunday there are more press conferences – if you win there are even more.

The Friday Five sessions can be entertaining. The five people chosen include team personnel and other F1 personalities as well as drivers, so the questions and topics are more varied. I've managed to be at most of the Pole Position press conferences after qualifying on Saturday afternoon. They have usually been good, though some journalists won't ask their questions there and then. They wait until the press conference is over and grab you separately in the hope of getting a scoop.

Because I speak Italian, French and English, I have to do more interviews in different languages than some drivers. With the Italians it seems half the questions are about Ferrari, which is funny. Even though my interest is with Williams I give them an opinion anyway. The British journalists are fairly polite, the French are more aggressive but not really a problem.

You end up becoming familiar with many of the journalists and you know what to expect. Most of them are highly professional and responsible, but there are a few who always want sensationalism. Others may never talk to you but they write silly things about you anyway. But really, I haven't had many problems with the media.

Compared to IndyCars there are many more media people in F1, but there is a tendency for them to look for the top stories among the top few teams. When there isn't much competition on the track there is even more competition among the journalists to find something to write about.

Sometimes the questions get very personal and that can be aggravating. Being in such a high-profile sport the only thing you can call your own is your private life. This is something I cherish and would prefer to keep it private. But that doesn't stop some people from asking you intimate questions.

QUESTIONS AND ANSWERS

By this stage of the season I had been interviewed dozens of times. Here are some typical examples of the questions that had to be dealt with...

Why do you use the word 'we' when talking about your racing?
"The main reason is that racing is a team effort and it would be conceited to use the word 'I' too often. If one person did all the work then it might be appropriate but there are more than 230 people in the Williams organisation and 'we' are all in it together – win or lose. Referring to the collective effort avoids the unseemly 'I won/they lost' syndrome – taking the credit for success while blaming the team for any lack of it. However, if a mistake is mine there is no hesitation to say 'I.'"

What are your personal strengths as a driver and as a person?
"I hate those questions. I don't like talking about myself. Okay, if you insist ... In the car maybe my strength is to be relaxed, which is important. You need to keep a cool head, to know when to be aggressive, when not to be, and so on. In my personal life maybe being happy and content with what I have, just being normal, is a strength.

I probably have lots of weaknesses. I am fairly intransigent. I don't like sitting around waiting for something. I spend so little time away from work – from racing and testing – that I just don't want to waste any time for stupid reasons. In my work I am used to some kind of precision, even if I am pretty messy myself, and I want things to be organized."

Unlike many drivers you don't spend much time in the F1 paddock. Are you a loner?
"I don't like to be in the paddock just to be in the paddock. I am here to work, so I work. If I have nothing to do, I go. The racetrack is like my office. Other people don't stay in the office when their work is finished."

For an F1 driver you have some unusual hobbies – playing musical instruments, building computers, roller-blading – and you wear very casual clothing. Do you feel different from other drivers?
"I don't think there is any set way for an F1 driver to be. Even if that was the case I wouldn't like to feel that I was obliged to conform. My job is driving F1 cars and I intend to do that without changing the way I am. Just as a businessman is expected to wear a suit and tie, the uniform which goes with my job is my driving suit. Away from work, whether you are a businessman or a racing driver, you do what you want and you dress the way you like. Some people may be suprised by the way I dress, but their surprise comes as a surprise to me. I have not consciously tried to be different from other drivers. I am simply being myself."

What has impressed you most about F1?
"It's difficult to say. IndyCar racing is not a small series. I was used to the cars, the speed and having many fans around. Of course, F1 is much more international. It's not big only in one country, it's big everywhere and the drivers have more exposure. But what I like about racing is the racing itself, not the stardom part of it. I could easily live without that."

Did you expect to have done so well as a newcomer to F1?
"The results so far correspond with what I was expecting. From the beginning I was aware that I was onto a good thing with Williams, a top team with a good car and a good engine. I was also conscious that my arrival in F1 coincided with a season when many of the top drivers had switched teams. That's not a situation that happens very often. I knew they would need a certain amount of time to get used to their new teams, so the cards were stacked in my favour. For some people, the only question mark was whether I was up to the task or not. But I had confidence in my ability. If you don't believe in yourself, then no one else will."

What is the main difficulty you have had to overcome so far this season?
"The restricted number of laps available during practice. It would be nice to be able to drive ten laps with no other aim than getting to know the track. With the number of laps restricted to just 30 per session, this is a luxury I cannot afford. After my first three laps I am already supposed to have got close to the limits of the car, with a view to working on the setup. For a newcomer this is a real handicap. Of course, it

doesn't apply to the circuits I was able to test on before the season began."

What gives you more personal satisfaction: a perfect qualifying lap or a top race result?

"It depends. A perfect qualifying lap feels great, though this year I haven't had one yet. But if you are fighting in a race it feels great as well. If you are leading all the time and win by 20 seconds, having driven without pressure, it can be boring. The interesting thing is to win having had a good battle – like the one I had with Michael Schumacher at the Nürburgring. That was fun. If you win by a considerable margin it maybe gives you some feeling of superiority, like an ego trip, but I don't care for that. If you are running in sixth place and within a few laps you make some good moves and overtake people, that can be very satisfying."

Has your experience in IndyCar racing been of any particular use to you?

"My experience was different to that of the majority of other drivers who have grown up with European racing. I came with a fresh approach. For example, Damon and I go with completely different setups concerning things like springs, shock absorbers, ride height, anti-roll bars, and so on. It would be impossible to transpose settings from one car to the other, and that doesn't make life easy for the team.

How closely do you work with your team mate?

"Apart from exchanging data, Damon and I rarely work together and this is a situation I am used to. In IndyCar racing even the teams with two drivers work separately. In our technical debriefs Damon and I don't share much information. I find that normal. Why should he reveal his secrets to me? I wouldn't reveal mine to him, and I certainly have more to learn from him than he does from me. We get along well as team mates, but we're both paid to win and we go about it differently."

Is your objective to help Damon win the championship or are you aiming to win it yourself?
"I race for myself and for the team. I understand that what matters to the team is winning, whoever the driver is, and the Constructors' Championship is what counts most for the team. However, a driver has got to think of himself. In some teams there is a Number 1 and a Number 2. That's not the case at Williams. Frank Williams doesn't expect me to help Damon. He expects me to win races and, if possible, the driving championship.

HUNGARIAN GRAND PRIX

HUNGARORING, HUNGARY, 11 AUGUST 1996

Standing on the top step of the victory podium for the third time this season was a very special occasion, beginning with the fact that our one-two finish clinched the Constructors' Championship for the team. This win was also more crucial in our battle for the Drivers' Championship, and it was especially satisfying to beat Damon at the Hungaroring, a circuit I didn't know and didn't expect to like.

Of course, you like any circuit where you win and the Hungaroring was enjoyable to drive on, at least by yourself. However, it is not so good for racing because there are hardly any places where you can overtake. It certainly keeps you busy, with hardly any straights to speak of, a lot of corners, some of them suprisingly quick, that come in rapid succession, and a track surface which is made tricky by the sand and dust that lie just off the racing line. While these challenges make it interesting, the confined nature of the circuit also causes traffic jams in the race, so getting a good grid position, and a good start, would be vital.

I prefer wide open circuits with quick corners, and find them easier to learn, so it was a pleasant surprise to be immediately competitive at the Hungaroring. The learning process was probably made easier when the slippery surface at first kept the speeds down during practice. With all the sand around it felt like we were at a beach! As the traffic cleaned up the surface the grip improved progressively, though the changing conditions made arriving at a realistic setup more difficult because it was like shooting at a moving target. Yet we were always on the pace and this had a lot to do with our new setup situation.

For the first time this season we used some setup ideas I had wanted to try for a long time. Before coming to Hungary we tried them out at the Nogaro circuit in France, which requires high downforce settings similar to the Hungaroring. The changes we made worked very well at the test session and even better in Hungary.

Qualifying was a good battle with Michael Schumacher and Damon.

We traded fastest laps, though my best one was spoiled when the car got completely sideways – from simply pushing too hard – and about half a second was lost. In the end the three of us were separated by just over a tenth of a second, with Michael's Ferrari in front of Damon and me. This meant I would start immediately behind Michael while Damon's side of the front row, off the racing line and in the dust and sand, would put him at a bit of a disadvantage on the first lap. As it turned out Damon had a poor start and fell behind some slower cars; his misfortune played right into our game plan.

I was determined to be very aggressive in this race and the car was obviously capable of matching my mood. For sure it was better than Michael's Ferrari, which was sliding all over the track as he pushed hard to keep the lead. The problem of overtaking him was solved when he went into the pits for his first stop. Meanwhile, our decision to make three pit stops for refuelling meant I was able to take advantage of the car being light and quickly open up a gap. Our first two pit stops were perfect, and by the time it became necessary to stop for the third time we were alone in front by over 20 seconds.

Unfortunately, half that lead was lost because of a delay replacing a rear wheel during our last pit stop. This was annoying, but from a racing point of view it was a bonus because it helped Damon get closer and set the stage for our exciting battle. When Michael's Ferrari had a mechanical failure, Damon took over second place and began pushing as hard as he could. This was a welcome wakeup call for me (and maybe for the fans), because until Damon came into the picture the race was becoming boring. But with his challenge came an adrenaline rush that certainly eliminated all boredom in the cockpit.

The last 15 laps were a real test for us both. Our cars were very evenly matched, if anything Damon's was slightly quicker, and we were both on the limit. My task was to avoid making a mistake under pressure, especially when lapping slower traffic, and the Hungaroring would do the rest – its tight configuration making it very difficult for Damon to overtake. And that's the way it ended, with our cars crossing the finish line just a few metres apart.

It had been a gruelling race in the heat, a real test of stamina, so it was a relief to see the chequered flag and then a delight to see how happy the team was. This race, in fact the whole season to date, had been a terrific team effort, not only from those who come to the races but also the test team and all the people back at the Williams factory. We are all racers at heart, and this is why we go racing: to win.

Having secured the team title we could now concentrate on the Drivers' Championship. Damon still had a 17 point lead, but scoring maximum points on an unfamiliar circuit gave me even more optimism for the next race. The Spa circuit, in Belgium, would also be new territory, but it has a reputation for being one of the greatest road racing circuits in the world and I was really looking forward to it. With another good result there and the final three races on circuits I knew fairly well the World Championship was still very much a possibility.

AT WORK IN THE OFFICE

For the difficult business of racing on a circuit like the Hungaroring, where you have to work very hard on every lap and there are 77 of them to be dealt with in the race, everything has to be right in the driver's 'office' – the cockpit. And just as a well organized office improves efficiency, a driver needs to have all the tools of his trade within easy reach and to feel comfortable sitting at his 'desk' for long periods of time.

Actually, an F1 driver's 'office' looks more like the cramped cockpit of a jet fighter, full of instruments and controls in a confined space. The cockpit of my Williams FW18 is so familiar it seems like a second home to me, and though it's not that easy to get into, it's quite comfortable once you're installed.

When you climb into the cockpit someone helps fasten your seat belts and you do the final adjustments on the shoulder straps yourself. The objective is to have the belts fit snugly so that you're firmly anchored in place. The more you move around in the cockpit the less you feel what's happening and the more tiring it gets. You have to be at one with the car, so that you can sense everything through every part of your body and translate those sensations into driving responses.

The seat fits very well because it's moulded to the shape of your body, but the comfort level is not so high because the carbon fibre seat is very hard. It has a thin covering of suede, but you certainly feel the bumps. The sides of the cockpit are close to your elbows, though the footwell is quite roomy. This can be a problem when the g-forces are high, so you have to learn to brace your legs and feet to keep them from banging the sides.

It's important to have your mirrors set exactly right so you can see as much as possible to the sides as well as behind. You need as wide a view as possible, so that even if you're not looking in the mirrors they are positioned in such a way that you become immediately aware of anything that pops into the corner of your eyes through peripheral vision.

Also for improved vision, the steering wheel is flat on top. The idea is that you can see over it, though I actually prefer a round wheel because you have more to work with – when controlling the car in a spin, for instance. On the steering wheel I keep my hands in the 'quarter to three' position. Full lock is less than 180 degrees, so it only takes a slight turn of the wheel to change direction.

Behind the steering wheel is the instrument panel, which helps you keep track of what's going on with the car, and also some controls which you can use to make adjustments. Directly in front of you is a liquid crystal display unit with a mode button for selecting different kinds of information to be displayed on the panel's three screens: your lap times, your speed-trap time, and so on.

On the right side of the LCD screens are four warning lights programmed to warn you of abnormal water or oil temperatures and pressures. On the left side of the screens are four shift lights that act like a rev counter – changing colour from green to yellow and then red when the engine reaches maximum revs – to remind you when it's time to shift gears. But when you become accustomed to the sound of the engine you can also use your ears to know when to shift. When you're shifting up or down through the gears you're also doing a mental count, but in case you lose track one reading on the display panel shows what gear you're in.

The gears are changed with the two paddles behind the spokes of the steering wheel. On my car the paddle on the left side is for the clutch, unlike the clutch on Damon's car which is operated from a conventional pedal on the floor. The paddle on the right side is the shifter, which I pull to downshift and push to upshift. In my IndyCars I also had a sequential shift, though it was done with a standard gearshift lever. I prefer sequential shifting because I became accustomed to it on motorbikes when I was a kid, and it's also handy to be familiar with sequential shifting to play video games successfully !

Four buttons in different colours, so you can easily pick them out in the heat of battle, are located on the steering wheel. The green radio button is only pushed when you want to speak to the pits. The radio intercom from the pit crew to the driver is always open. The red button, which kills the engine, would only be used in emergencies, such as having a sticking throttle. The yellow button puts the car in neutral, when you're in first or second gear, so the engine won't stall in the pits.

The white button on the steering wheel has two functions, depending on which gear you're in. In a low gear the white button is a rev limiter which you push on when you're coming into the pits to prevent exceeding the pit lane speed limit. In Spain I forgot to push the white button and it cost me a lot of money – I was fined for speeding. In a higher gear the white button activates a small pump connected to your drinks bottle. If you want a drink you put the tube inside your helmet into your mouth and press the white button, though I seldom take a drink during a race.

I've never had to use the fire extinguisher switch, on the upper right-hand corner of the instrument panel, but a couple of times this season the extinguisher came on anyway. Once, during practice in France, we were adding fuel in the pits and the extinguisher cable was accidentally activated. There was fire-retardant powder everywhere, including in my face, and we had to do a major cleanup. Fortunately, I've never had a fire to deal with in the cockpit, but it's very reassuring to know the extinguisher is there should you need it.

There are other buttons and switches which I seldom use, including a gearbox isolating switch and a gearbox strategy switch, and the throttle sensitivity adjustor is locked on. I have used the air/fuel mixture adjustment to conserve fuel, and the brake balance bar, located on the left side of the instrument panel, is used frequently.

With the brake balance bar you can change the braking emphasis between the front and rear brakes. You use this a lot because the braking capabilities change as the brake pads wear and you have to adjust the balance. Even a tiny adjustment can make a big difference. The effect is similar to what bicycle riders do with the levers on the handlebars, applying more or less pressure on the front or rear brakes.

My feet have only two pedals to deal with, the brakes and the accelerator, and I keep both of them positioned as if they are extensions of the pedals. Having the clutch on the steering wheel means that at least I can never make a mistake between the brake and the clutch. My left foot is reserved for braking and I always keep it just resting on the pedal, without applying pressure until it's needed. The accelerator pedal is controlled with the right foot and is very sensitive to the touch. If you floor it you take off like a shot. If you release it you immediately slow down as if you are braking.

Since the name of the game is speed the accelerator is an important control, but you wouldn't get far with that speed if you weren't able to back it up by means of all the other stuff in the cockpit.

CHAPTER FOURTEEN

BELGIAN GRAND PRIX

SPA–FRANCORCHAMPS, BELGIUM, 25 AUGUST 1996

Finishing second on my first visit to one of the most challenging circuits in the world might be considered a satisfactory result. But after starting from pole position at Spa, then losing the lead during an unfortunate communication problem, it was disappointing not to have won the Belgian Grand Prix.

All season long I had been looking forward to racing here and it certainly lived up to my expectations. It really is one of the greatest tracks anywhere. It's too bad there aren't more of them, because the pleasure you get from driving at places like this is why you become a racing driver in the first place.

If you love real road-racing it doesn't get much better than Spa, whether you're a fan or a driver. Watching F1 cars sweep through the picturesque landscape at very high speed is one of the great spectacles in motor sport, and the view from the cockpit is just as good. It's a tremendous thrill to take Spa on the limit, going flat out around its many quick corners and keeping up the momentum as you climb up and down the steep hills. The combination of the wide-open configuration of the circuit and the quite long lap enables you to get into a smooth rhythm and feel that you're really expressing yourself behind the wheel. Besides the sheer pleasure of the sensation of speed there is a feeling of accomplishment that is wonderfully satisfying.

In some of the corners at Spa the enormous g-forces are equivalent to those on the superspeedways in IndyCar racing. The most famous section of the circuit, Eau Rouge, is fantastic. When you approach it you're going flat out downhill and all you can see in front of you is a wall that appears to be going straight up. You have to climb that wall, and change direction while you're doing it. The strange thing is that even when you think you're on the limit you can go even faster because the faster you go the more stable the car becomes. It's a tremendous thrill.

Before coming to Spa I did some homework. I watched a

videotape of Ayrton Senna on one of his great qualifying laps, and I also played a new video game which gives a quite realistic impression of the track. It may sound like a childish way to prepare for such serious business, but the game did help me learn the basics of the circuit layout. Spa is one of the longest circuits, and for a newcomer, because of all the complicated challenges you have to deal with over the 6.974 kilometres, by the time you get to the end of one lap you could easily forget the details of what went on before.

"Jacques made quite a story for himself on Saturday as it was the first time he had been to Spa, the most challenging of all the tracks he will visit this season. His pole position effort was a terrific performance."

FRANK WILLIAMS *(Team owner)*

In the video game my best time was only good enough for something like 18th, but in real life, in a Williams Renault, I managed to get pole position. This was very pleasing, considering I had never driven at Spa, but on the other hand my expectations were high. Besides the enjoyment of driving on a terrific circuit there was also extra incentive to perform at the maximum to continue the fight for the championship with Damon. Apart from the first race of the season, where I also got pole, Damon had usually outqualified me. Sometimes his time was only fractions of a second quicker, but that can be important, especially at the start, in determining the outcome of a race.

It nearly always rains sometime over the weekend at Spa, and sure enough there was a shower just after I set the fastest time. Then it began to clear up and Jock Clear was worried that somebody might go quicker when the track dried out again. I bet Jock that our time would stand and he lost. Now, at the last race of the season (in Japan) he would have to shave his head!

There was no way that Jock could back out of his obligation because the whole team heard us making the bet over the radio. We had no trouble communicating at this point, when we were parked in the garage, but a later conversation over the radio proved to be less successful.

Being quickest again in the pre-race warm-up was an encouraging rehearsal for the afternoon's work, which was unlikely to be easy since Damon and Michael Schumacher were second and third on the grid. As it turned out, Damon had a slower start and it was Michael I had to contend with.

Our car was slightly quicker than his Ferrari, and it needed to be because Michael was performing at his best on a circuit where he has had some of his greatest races. The job of keeping him behind became more difficult when a brake imbalance caused the front wheels to lock up on several occasions. This wore flat spots on the tyres which created a vibration and also contributed to some understeer that was worrying on Spa's quicker corners. Dealing with these problems while pushing as hard as possible to protect the lead made Spa even more exciting!

Still, everything went well and I was able to keep ahead of Michael for the first part of the race. Then, when the safety car came out after an accident, Jock Clear's voice came over the radio and I couldn't understand what he was saying. With the field slowing down and bunching up behind the safety car it was important to quickly make a pit stop for fuel and fresh tyres. Michael did so immediately, but it took us another lap to sort out our communication mix-up and by then Michael had taken over the lead.

Jock had been telling me to come in to the pits and I had been requesting the same thing – but the radio wasn't working properly. Obviously, it was the right time to stop, and as the driver I might have made my own decision, but when I didn't hear Jock's confirmation our stop was delayed and it probably cost us the race.

After we got back on track and racing resumed, it was harder to chase Michael than it had been to stay in front of him. Following in the slipstream of his Ferrari the downforce on my car was reduced, which meant the front tyres had less grip and the understeer was more pronounced. With the front end threatening to break away at any time on the quickest corners, Spa became even more of a challenge.

But it was important to keep up the pressure and score the maximum possible points because Damon was on his way to a fifth place finish. So I kept pushing until just near the end of the race, when I backed off a bit because I thought I heard a strange noise coming from the exhaust system. It may have only been my imagination, but I was taking no chances after the setback caused by our earlier hearing problem.

The satisfaction from having performed well in Belgium was offset by the fact that it only reduced Damon's lead in the championship by four points, and to overcome his 13 point advantage there was even more work to do in the remaining three races. Yet the job seemed easier after having raced well enough to win on the greatest circuit of them all.

A ROLLER COASTER RIDE

Spa is an amazing place to go racing, like a really wild roller coaster ride that takes your breath away. By the time you've completed even one quick lap, at an average speed of over 225 kilometres per hour, you've had the driving experience of a lifetime.

The first challenge is La Source, a right-hand hairpin which you approach under heavy braking, to come down from about 270 kph in fifth gear to about 60 kph in first gear. It's the slowest corner but also quite tricky, and several different lines are possible as you put the power down on the exit. A metal drainage grating runs across the road here and as you cross it you have to be careful with your acceleration, to avoid wasted wheelspin or losing control and slamming into the barrier on the left. You shave the barrier as close as possible and then you really step on it, flicking up through the gears into sixth as you go down the steep hill. By the time you reach the bottom you're moving at nearly 300 kph and you have to get your head in gear for Spa's biggest challenge: Eau Rouge.

Just before you begin the climb through Eau Rouge you cross a bridge (over a stream with red-coloured water that gives the corner its name) where the car bottoms out very heavily. The g-forces are pressing down on your helmet, the underside of the chassis bangs hard on the surface of the track, sending sparks flying and the car jumping sideways, you're fighting the wheel, hanging on as best you can, with your vision blurred from all the bouncing, the engine screaming more loudly than ever in your ears, and you have to keep your mind set on doing what seems impossible: taking Eau Rouge flat out.

I first decided to try this during practice on Saturday

morning before qualifying. You have to make the conscious decision to do it. You have to break through a barrier that's mental as well as physical. It's similar to the corners on a superspeedway oval where you have to force yourself to go quicker when your survival instincts are demanding that you should back off. The mind-over-matter theory of faster cornering is based on the fact that the quicker you go the more downforce you create, so the car sticks better and you can go even faster.

When you're going flat out through Eau Rouge it seems like you're climbing straight up into the sky. You're turning left and right while the car gets very heavy and flattens itself down on the track, because of the extra downforce, but the adhesion is precarious and the car skips sideways – at about 275 kph. Even if you feel on the verge of disaster you have to imagine your right foot is bolted flat to the floor and you can't lift off. You have to tell yourself 'My foot is not coming up' and you hang in there, getting more and more tense. You stop breathing, you start closing your eyes...No you don't close your eyes. They stay wide open – with fear!...But when you're safely through Eau Rouge your eyes blink quite rapidly.

The first time you successfully take Eau Rouge flat out you wonder if you should tempt fate again. You feel as if you've been absolutely on the ragged edge and maybe you were lucky to make it. The main difficulty with being so much on the limit through here is that you're less in control of a situation in which the car is fully stressed. But so are you. You're getting banged around a lot, the maximum g-forces are pushing and pulling your body and you can't react as quickly to any problems.

A lot of what happens here depends on instinct and blind faith in your own capabilities. Part way up the hill the car is out on the curb at the right and you have to turn left again. You're looking ahead but you can't see the exit. All you can see is the wall of asphalt in front of you and the red and white kerb beside you. You have to guess where you're going and you just hang on until the landscape returns to normal and you can see a long straight looming up ahead.

From Eau Rouge you climb steadily up to Les Combes, a right-hander where you need to brake heavily from over 300 kph to about half that speed. It's important to get Les Combes right to set yourself up for the succession of bends which follow. You can develop a good rhythm here as you sweep through Malmédy, where you don't need to brake, just ease up a bit, and on the steep descent to Rivage you build up speed to about 250 kph.

Rivage was my least favourite corner at Spa. It's off camber, sloping to the left as you're turning right, and our car was short of grip here because of our setup. Understeer made every lap frustrating. You just sat there, putting on full lock and waiting, and waiting, for the car to turn. Below Rivage, at the next left-hander, taken in third gear at about 150 kph, there was a similar delay in steering response. To compensate you had to actually start turning before you wanted to, not something I personally enjoy. This corner was also off camber and slippery and on a quick lap if you braked hard to help the turn-in process you would get sideways.

The aggravation of these slower parts of Spa are soon forgotten when you arrive at Pouhon, one of the most rewarding corners on the circuit. You slow from about 280 kph with a small tap on the brakes and turn into Pouhon, and then you accelerate all the way through it, which is a great feeling. You're sloping downhill and just when you think you're finished with Pouhon it goes even sharper left and you get really close to the outer kerb. By this time you're flat out and generating g-forces about four times the force of gravity. It's really exhilarating.

The right and left turns at Fagnes are taken in two stages. The first part is very grippy and you're going uphill as you brake very hard, slowing from nearly 300 kph to about 160 kph. Then you accelerate very hard but only briefly, before slowing down for the second part of the turn, where you fly over a hump while trying to maintain control on a very slippery surface which is also off camber.

After Fagnes you accelerate up through the gears to Stavelot, another corner that you take in two stages that swing you around through 90 degrees. You take the first part at about 150 kph in third and in the second part you're flat out in fourth, at about 230 kph. Stavelot is fairly straightforward but satisfying and exciting nonetheless.

Blanchimont, a long sweeping right hand turn, is taken flat out at well over 300 kph. The combination of the high speed while you're turning made it feel like a corner on an oval circuit, and the 4g's Blanchimont produces are also similar to those on an IndyCar superspeedway. Also familiar to me was the lack of runoff area here, with the barrier right beside the track. But if you lose control on a corner like this, hitting a nearby wall, providing you hit it a glancing blow, can dissipate some of the energy of a crash. Fortunately, I didn't have to put this theory to the test.

After the thrill of Blanchimont you have to brake very heavily to negotiate the worst part of Spa: the Bus Stop chicane. It was put there for reasons of safety, but swerving left and right at about 80 kph is no fun at all. The chicane is not natural like the rest of the circuit, which is mostly made up of real public roads, and besides spoiling your rhythm the chicane seems against the spirit of Spa.

Anyway, you're soon finished with the boring Bus Stop and a few hundred metres later, as you accelerate flat out across the start/finish line, you've got a big grin on your face again because you're on another lap of Spa.

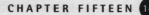

ITALIAN GRAND PRIX

MONZA, ITALY, 11 SEPTEMBER 1996

After finishing seventh and not scoring any points in the Italian Grand Prix, some people wanted to know why I wasn't more disappointed or angry. The answer was that I had been working off my frustrations by driving hard for about 50 laps despite having a crippled car. Dealing with the severe handling problems was exhausting and had a calming influence. Besides, any road rage would have to be directed at yours truly, since the problems stemmed from my driving error in the early laps. A similar situation, hitting a tyre barrier, caused Damon to spin out of the race. Though our misfortunes meant it was a pointless weekend for our team it kept our battle for the drivers' championship alive.

Before this race we had a test session at the Paul Ricard circuit in France and then a few days off at home in Monaco. After catching up on some training and looking after the usual domestic chores in the flat, I organized a game of 'Dungeons and Dragons' with some of my friends. There were eight of us, and we became so wrapped up in the game that we played for 18 hours over the weekend. It was a great way to cut off from the real world and forget about racing.

Our trip to Italy began pleasantly enough, with an enjoyable drive up from the Mediterranean coast to Monza, just outside Milan. The Autodromo di Monza was the scene of some of my first racing adventures, in the Italian Formula 3 series. In those days it was still one of the great tracks, with high average speeds, some really challenging corners and lots of places for overtaking. Since then changes have been made to improve safety, including chopping up some of the quicker corners with chicanes. Having to slow down for the chicanes destroyed the rhythm that used to be so rewarding at Monza, though it is still a fun place to drive an F1 car, as we found out when we had a test session there before this season began.

When we went out for practice on Friday we found new cement kerbs had been installed in the chicanes, and as soon as we started going quickly they caused problems. For a fast lap you have to really attack the chicanes, which includes hitting the kerbs, and before long some of them began to break up. I found this out the hard way when a car in front of me dislodged a piece of cement that flew up and broke the front wing on my car. It could have been worse, it could have hit my helmet, but it was clear that something had to be done to stop the kerb-hopping. As a temporary solution it was decided to put tyre barriers in front of the kerbs. The drivers were consulted about this, but some of us had reservations about what would happen if we hit the tyres during the race.

Sure enough, the tyre barriers did cause a lot of problems and, in fact, were a major factor in determining the outcome of the Italian Grand Prix. Certainly, they ruined my race, but in one way I was lucky to even be in it, after a very serious incident on Saturday morning.

I was on a quick lap, travelling at 325 kilometres per hour down one of Monza's straights, when a much slower car moved in front of me and forced me onto the grass. My car spun out of control and slammed into a guard rail. Fortunately some of the momentum was scrubbed off in the spin and the car wasn't too badly damaged. But it was a frightening situation and one that could have ended in disaster. I was extremely angry about being put off the road in such a way, even if it wasn't intentional.

It was also aggravating to have to miss the rest of the practice session, when we should have been perfecting the setup for qualifying. Still, after repairs the car felt reasonably good, considering what it had been through, and we managed to set a time good enough for second on the grid, behind Damon. In the pre-race warm-up session the car felt solid, though for some reason it lacked straightline speed compared to Damon's. Our qualifying positions meant our battle for the drivers' championship would continue from the front row of the starting grid. As it turned out it didn't go much further than that.

The start was a bit erratic, with everyone jockeying for position, including Damon who started to squeeze me over to the pit lane wall on the right side of the track. We managed to avoid contact, but there was a lot of traffic still bunched together as we approached the first chicane. I found myself with no room to take the conventional line, and to avoid causing an accident I had to cut across the chicane. There was no penalty for taking a shortcut because I hadn't overtaken anyone. In fact, overtaking would have been difficult because the car felt sluggish again, as it had in the warmup. On the straights going up through the gears it was as if there was a wall in front of me, and by the third lap I had dropped back to fifth place.

It was then that I clipped the tyre barrier at one of the chicanes. It was simply a mistake in judgement and seemed like only a light tap, but it was enough to bend some front suspension components. The handling became very strange, it seemed as if one front wheel was higher than the other, and obviously it was ruining the tyres because after a few laps bits of rubber began flying off them. We had planned one pit stop, but had to make three of them to replace the worn tyres. The combined effect of the various difficulties put us well out of contention but others were having problems so it was important to keep pushing in the hope of collecting some points. In the end half the field failed to finish, but enough of the frontrunners remained to keep us out of the points.

Many of the retirements were, like Damon's, caused by cars hitting the tyres at the kerbs and a better solution must be found before we race at Monza again. In the more immediate future there were two races remaining in the 1996 season – two more chances to do something about Damon's 13 point lead in the championship.

OFF TRACK

While our Italian Grand Prix was a very busy one, the actual race only took me about 80 minutes. However, there is a lot more to a Grand Prix weekend than simply driving the car.

Thursday...

Thursday afternoon is when our race weekend officially begins, but we often arrive at the circuit sooner, to have more time to become acclimatized to the mostly new environments facing me this season. If the circuit is too far to drive from Monaco I sometimes take a flight late on Wednesday. When we're racing outside Europe we arrive on Monday or Tuesday to give us extra time to get over jet lag.

Wherever we are in the world the paddocks are similar in that there are the same motorhomes and the same people, though there are differences in the ambience within the paddocks. Some of them are nicer than others, with more open space and sometimes even some green grass, while others are on a paved surface in cramped areas so it feels like being in a crowded town. I prefer the open countryside type of paddock, which is why I think the impossibly crowded conditions at the Monaco Grand Prix are the worst.

On Thursday the first thing I do is go to the garage to see Jock Clear and the guys and go over whatever points might be relevant to the weekend. We exchange ideas and build up the chemistry to get ourselves into racing mode. On Thursday we also try to schedule as many interviews as possible from the requests that are made by the media, so the rest of the weekend can be devoted to concentrating on driving.

After spending at least three hours in the paddock I head

back to the hotel and have dinner at about 8 o'clock. My routine on a race weekend is quite rigid and everything I do is intended to help get me into a racing mindset. My girlfriend or anyone else who might be travelling with me knows this and accepts it. I enjoy having company and try to be sociable, but racing has to come first. Thursday to Sunday have to be done my way.

On Thursday night I try to get to bed by 22.00 or 23.00, maybe reading a bit until I fall asleep. Going to sleep is easier now than when I began racing and was less sure of my capabilities and perhaps worried more about racing. Each year, with improving results, sleep has come easier so it seems that success acts like a sedative. Fortunately, I haven't had much trouble falling asleep since I've been in F1.

Friday...
On Friday I get up early enough to allow for getting through traffic to the circuit, and usually arrive in the paddock at least 90 minutes before we have to go out on the track for practice. We eat breakfast in the Williams motorhome, usually with Craig and Jock. Breakfast is my most important meal of the day and I have a big one – eggs, muesli, maybe some toast and peanut butter with milk to drink.

Immediately after practice there is always a round of interviews and press conferences, so that you don't have lunch until mid-afternoon – and we usually eat in the office in one of the team trucks, while we're debriefing. If things are going well the debrief is shorter; it's usually followed by some public relations work for the sponsors and we don't leave the track until around 19.00. Back at the hotel we have a quick meal and try to get to bed as early as possible to rest up for Saturday, when it becomes busier than ever.

Saturday...
On Saturday we have breakfast at the track at 07.30 and are on the track at 09.00 to begin practice. Between then and the end of qualifying I spend most of the time either in the car or in the garage. If you're in the top three in qualifying you have to attend a pole position press conference right after you get out of the car.

You don't have time for a proper lunch, so you gulp something down quickly, because there are appearances to be made in the sponsors' suites for up to an hour. After that you try to get a bit more lunch before you meet the media for more interviews, and then go back to the team for another debriefing session. Often it's 19.00 or 20.00 before you leave the circuit and sometimes there are appearances to be made away from the track, before you get back to the hotel.

It's always non-stop on Saturday. Cramming so much into the day can have a negative influence on the driving side, but it's the way things are done in F1. By the end of the day you've spent about 12 hours with your head in high gear, being jerked around, eating too quickly and not enough, with no time to relax. You are usually exhausted and at this point it's important to have a good evening meal, when you can also laugh and talk about anything other than racing.

Sometimes you're too wound up to fall asleep quickly, but that can also be productive. When you're lying in bed and calmed down and there are no distractions this is one of the best times for coming up with ideas for improving your racing.

You only hope you can remember your ideas when you wake up in the morning! In the same way driving to a race from Monaco instead of flying can be a productive time for thinking about what you might do on the track.

Sunday...
Sunday morning is another early start because you have to allow for heavier traffic going to the circuit. You should be there two hours before the warmup which is usually at 09.30. Even though it's race day, the most critical part of the weekend, I'm usually quite relaxed. In fact, I'm relaxed every morning because I'm too tired to be tense! At breakfast in the motorhome we talk over things with Jock. Overnight we both have probably come up with some ideas.

After the warm-up, you get out of the car and have about one hour to discuss things with the team before you go to the drivers' briefing in the race control centre. There we're given a general briefing about the procedures for the race and about anything new that might be planned, and if a driver has any suggestions or questions this is when they are heard. It's usually a good exchange of views. You find out what the drivers think, what can and cannot be done, and compromises are often made.

Then there is the drivers' parade, which I don't enjoy so much because it usually causes problems with my contact lenses. As we drive around the circuit in an open car there is always a lot of dust and wind which dries out the contacts, and they are very uncomfortable afterwards. Maybe I should wear goggles.

I don't mind seeing the fans and waving to them, and

usually we get a good reception. But in the parade at Monza Damon and I, riding in the same car as usual, were booed and given the finger by some of the Ferrari maniacs. We had fun accusing each other of provoking the negative reaction. You keep smiling and waving all the time and it's usually fun. The people are there to see a show, and when you get large groups together it's normal that the collective mentality goes down a few notches.

For some reason there was no drivers' parade in Montreal so I missed the experience of appearing in front of my home fans. It's natural for the home fans to cheer for the local hero, but even in Germany Michael Schumacher's fans were cheering all of us, though their habit of throwing firecrackers can be a bit disconcerting. One of the best parades was in Brazil where we all went around the track in the same truck. The fans were cheering for us as a group and this was nicer. Nobody felt left out.

After the parade you have to go and visit sponsors and their guests in the hospitality suites. By the time you have fulfilled all your obligations you have about one hour to get ready to race – and you haven't had lunch yet, or the pre-race briefing with the team. So you have to quickly gobble down some food while you're talking and then you rush to get into the car.

I must admit I'm not too happy with the way Sundays are organized. Suddenly, after all the coming and going, you find yourself in the cockpit, and you're not sure about the car, you probably have indigestion from eating too quickly and it's often an uncomfortable time. The weekend up until this point has been fairly hectic, but it doesn't make sense to cram so much extracurricular stuff into the short time on Sunday, to the point that you're often less than ideally prepared for the most important part of the weekend: the race. But this is the way things are done and you have to accept it.

Sometimes, about half an hour before getting into the car, there is time for a quick massage from Erwin, our physiotherapist, and then it takes me about 15 minutes to get properly fitted into the cockpit. Mostly at this time I'm fairly calm, unless the preceding obligations have taken up even more time than usual, which can make you hyper simply because you haven't been able to do everything you need to do, like go to the toilet!

Anyway, you soon forget about everything else because you become extremely busy. At 13.30 we drive out of the pits and line up on the starting grid. In the next half hour you have a final chat with the team and then you focus inwardly, concentrating on the task at hand. And at 14.00 you go racing.

After the race the strongest desire is to leave the circuit and go home. You've done your job, the climax is over and you've shut down mentally. You were on a high and now you've come down. During the race your body builds up endorphins and adrenaline, and when the high from them subsides at the chequered flag you're feeling fatigued and somewhat negative, especially if you've had a bad race. You don't feel like doing anything except leaving. Even if you win, the feeling of euphoria is very brief and you just want to get away from it all. The only thing is, the more successful you are the longer you have to stay around.

As soon as you get out of the car you're surrounded by officials and quickly rushed up to make an appearance on the podium, where you listen to the national anthems being played, receive your trophy and then observe the custom of spraying the champagne. Though I don't like getting champagne in the face because it irritates my eyes with the contact lenses, it's all part of the fun and I can spray with the best of them. But for me, after working hard in the race, having a sip of the champagne is more important than spraying it.

Following the podium appearance you're dragged away to attend a succession of press conferences. Up to this point you haven't yet seen anybody from the team, and you're left feeling that something is missing from the human side of racing. Later, it's even harder to share any success with the team because by the time you get back to the garage everybody is busy packing up to leave the circuit. It may seem strange to feel isolated from humanity when you're surrounded by so much of it, but that's often the way it is on a Grand Prix weekend.

PORTUGUESE GRAND PRIX

ESTORIL, PORTUGAL, 22 SEPTEMBER 1996

The main goal in the Portuguese Grand Prix was to score at least four points more than Damon, which would keep my world championship hopes alive. Achieving that goal by winning the race was very satisfying and having such an exciting time doing it doubled the pleasure. This was not only my most important win of the season so far, it was also the most fun.

I t helped that this crucial race was on a circuit where we had done a lot of testing. Estoril is for the most part tight and twisty, though there are some high speed turns where you can really reduce your lap times if you keep your foot down. You have to do this in qualifying because there aren't many places to overtake and a good grid position is vital. Our thorough knowledge of the circuit meant we had the qualifying setup exactly the way we wanted it, and everything went well in the driving department too. The only problem was that in qualifying Damon was nine thousandths of a second quicker when a shower of rain near the end of the session prevented any chance of beating his time.

It was really frustrating to come so close to pole position. According to our Renault engineers the time difference between us was the equivalent of just 75 centimetres on the track. The only consolation was that on several previous occasions when Damon had the advantage in qualifying it had still been possible to beat him in the race. And that's how it worked out in Portugal, though it didn't get off to a promising start.

By the time we had sorted ourselves out on the first lap Damon was well in the lead and I was back in fourth place, behind Jean Alesi and Michael Schumacher. At this point our prospects looked a bit grim. The only option was to keep racing as hard as possible, and before long it paid off.

Before the race I mentioned to the guys in our team that one corner reminded me of an IndyCar oval, where it's possible to overtake a car on the outside. This is seldom done in F1 racing, and the guys said if I tried such a crazy move they would have to come out and pick me out of the guard rail. So the first thing I said on the radio after I passed Michael was: 'You see, it worked!'

As we approached the corner on the sixteenth lap a slower car in front of Michael forced him to ease off a bit and I immediately moved right up beside him, on the outside, where he wasn't expecting an attack. The element of surprise was important, and Michael said later he didn't even see me until our wheels were almost touching. I hadn't noticed this because I was too busy finishing off the manoeuvre.

"Obviously, I was surprised when he overtook me. I looked in my mirror and couldn't find him – then suddenly he was beside me. It was a scary moment, but we got away with it."
MICHAEL SCHUMACHER *(Ferrari driver)*

It was extremely close, but he was very fair and left just enough room to squeeze by. With Michael you know he is always in complete command of his car and I probably wouldn't have tried such a risky move on a lesser driver. Michael said it was fun for him and it certainly was for me. It's what racing is all about and if you can make one move like this in a race you're happy, no matter where you finish.

Even at this stage of the race it seemed that Damon was uncatchable. But after our second pit stops the gap between us became progressively reduced. I was able to get fairly close until the reduced downforce in his slipstream caused my tyres to go off and the car started sliding around.

When Damon went into the pits for his third stop the team

signalled that I was to come in the next time around. I began to push really hard, taking advantage of the clean air for the rest of the lap. Even the trip into the pit lane was right on the edge of adhesion and I had to lock up the brakes to stop for the waiting pit crew. They were very brave and didn't budge and their pit work was superbly quick. Changing all four wheels and adding fuel took only 8 seconds. A split-second longer could have made the difference because when we came back out on the track we were just a few metres in front of Damon.

Our first and second positions meant the necessary four points over Damon were in the bag, but it was important to keep pushing as hard as possible to create an insurance gap for when we hit slower traffic. Everything went smoothly, the car was perfect and even late in the race it was capable of setting the fastest lap of the day. The twisty Estoril circuit is very demanding physically, but the momentum from driving nearly as hard as in qualifying created a euphoria that overpowered any feelings of fatigue. And standing on the top step of the podium was the happiest possible ending to a great race.

The next race, in Japan, would be the last one of the season – the final opportunity to challenge for the championship. Damon still had a nine point lead but the winner in Japan would get ten points. I would just have to try to win again and let the rest of the points fall where they may.

ON TRACK

Over a Grand Prix weekend, including racing for up to two hours on Sunday, the track is open to F1 cars for up to six hours. Of course, we're not out there that long because on Friday and Saturday the rules restrict us to a certain number of laps.

Practising...

On Friday there are two hours of practice, divided into two separate 60-minute sessions with a one-hour interval between them. The day is mostly devoted to setting the car up, though for newcomers like me practice on Friday is also spent learning unfamiliar tracks.

We start with only a lap or two to check things out on the car. Then we come into the pits, where we usually sit for half an hour because you are limited to a total of only 30 laps in the two sessions and you don't want to waste them on a 'green' track. So everybody plays the waiting game, hoping that others will go out and clean up the track surface and lay down some rubber to provide better adhesion. If there was no limit on the laps everybody would be out more often. Finally, in the last half hour, everybody goes out and we usually run about 15 laps in each session.

Because of all the waiting around Fridays can be a bit boring. After getting installed in the cockpit, having all the belts done up and getting comfortable, I prefer to sit in the car. You sit there waiting for some action and getting annoyed at the inactivity. Sometimes at private test sessions there are lengthy lulls while equipment is being changed, and I may doze off a bit until it's time to drive again. But on a Grand Prix weekend you have to stay alert and be ready to go at a moment's notice.

During the one-hour break between practice sessions I change into a clean set of underwear, talk to Jock and hang around the garage until we go out again. There is usually more traffic in the final hour of practice, with everyone working harder on their setups. Still, most teams treat Friday as a test session and the real action isn't until tomorrow.

On Saturday the practice routine is similar to Friday, though there are two 45-minute sessions, with a half-hour break in between. Most of Saturday practice, especially the second session, is devoted to setting the car up for qualifying, and once again we have a maximum of only 30 laps. Even though you're aware of the urgency of preparing for qualifying, you're always conscious of saving laps and not wanting to waste them.

Qualifying...

On most tracks the one-hour qualifying session is second only to the race in importance, because overtaking in the race is so difficult. The pressure is pretty high, because you are limited to only 12 laps in qualifying. We might have two, three or four runs on new sets of tyres. With each set of tyres there are only a couple of laps when you can get the most out of them. Every run has to be on the limit and you can't afford to throw away any laps. This means more sitting in the car, waiting for the right moment to go out. While we're there Jock and I are talking on the radio, watching the weather and track conditions and looking for gaps in traffic so we can go out at the most opportune time.

When going for a quick time I give myself a pep talk to build up the aggression level. It happens progressively, beginning just before going out on the warm-up lap and continuing until the car crosses the start/finish line. During the quick lap you have to give everything you have – all the energy and emotion – so that sometimes it seems equivalent to what you put into a whole race.

PATRIOTIC POWER

As a driver you represent your country and I'm proud to carry the Canadian flag at the F1 circuits around the world.

EXTRA PRESSURE
*The expectations of the
Canadian fans created extra
pressure to do well in my
home race. They seemed
pleased with my second
place finish.*

TROPHIES COLLECTED
*Included among the awards
collected so far was the Lou
Marsh Trophy, given to
Canada's athlete of the year.*

TEAM MATES AND RIVALS
*By the half-way point in the
season my team mate Damon
Hill and I were first and
second in the championship.*

ACCIDENT RECOVERY

Considering my big crash in qualifying, second place was a good result in the French Grand Prix.

BACK ON TRACK

My second F1 victory, at the British Grand Prix, was overdue and opportune since it tightened up the championship battle with Damon.

COMPUTER ASSISTANCE
I love computers, but when it comes to setting up a car I think they should be mostly used as backup to the driver's feedback.

HEAD TO HEAD
For the Hungarian Grand Prix our technical director Patrick Head let me try some setup ideas of my own. The experiment was a success and we won.

SPLIT-SECOND TEAMWORK
Throughout the season our pit stops were timed to perfection but a rare communications mix-up left us second best in Belgium.

HUNGARIAN HAPPINESS

This win helped clinched the Constructors' Championship for the team. Now, with four races to go, Damon and I were free to concentrate on the Driver's Championship.

 Throttle map selector

 Brake balance: adjusts front/rear balance

Radio button: communication with engineers

Limiter: pitlane speed limiter/drinks button

Auto neutral: automatically selects neutral from either first or second gear

Cut-out: 'kills' engine

MODE **Mode:** switches dashboard display to show information on various components

MISSION CONTROL CENTRE

Surrounding you in the cockpit of an F1 car are all the instruments and controls you need to stay on course while you fight your racing battles.

© Russell Lewis

POINTLESS WEEKEND
My Italian Grand Prix went off course from the beginning. Damon also hit trouble so at least our championship battle would continue.

FRIGHTENING EXPERIENCE
Being forced off the road at 325 kph in Italy could easily have ended in disaster. Instead, it ended in extreme anger.

INCIDENT AFTERMATH
After spinning out of control my car slammed into a guardrail. After it was repaired we still managed second in qualifying.

KEEPING PACE
Training isn't often possible on a race weekend, but if you can fit in a quick run, and get a suntan at the same time, you're ahead of the game.

FLYING HIGH
Skiing is a great way of staying in shape and when you're skiing fast the requirements, and thrills, are similar to to driving a racing car.

TIGHT SQUEEZE
In the last race of the season one of us would be the 1996 World Champion, yet Damon and I were still enjoying ourselves.

DOUBLE THE FUN
Winning in Portugal was doubly satisfying because it required a very close overtaking manouevre on Michael and it set the stage for a final showdown with Damon.

GAME OVER
In Japan, a wheel fell off the car and my first F1 season ended in a cloud of dust. Still, finishing second in the championship was a great incentive to do better next time.

A HUGE DISAPPOINTMENT
An inauspicious start to the 1997 season in Melbourne as I'm squeezed off the track at the first bend. My race had lasted only 300 metres.

BACK ON TRACK
I came away from the 1997 Brazilian Grand Prix with pole position, fastest race lap, and a great victory.

You're tensed up and not nearly as relaxed as when you're racing. You just have to go for it – braking later, turning into corners quicker and really attacking the circuit. The objective is to go faster than ever before. Sometimes you reach a point where you find new limits beyond your expectations. When this happened at Spa it was hugely satisfying and my pole position lap there was a highlight of my season. But having a perfect lap is rare, and even if you get a good grid position you usually feel you could have done better in qualifying.

Warming up...

In the half-hour warm-up session on Sunday morning there is usually only time for six or seven worthwhile laps, not enough to thoroughly test anything new. You just have time to check things over and try the setup with the car on full tanks. Normally the temperatures are cooler in the warm-up than they will be in the afternoon so it's harder to get an exact indication of how the car will perform in the race.

Racing...

Getting a good start is crucial because, with the difficulty of overtaking, the outcome of the race can be decided in the first few seconds. I've worked hard on my starts because in Formula 3 I used to get too excited and stall the car, or rev the engine too high and get wheelspin. Ever since then I've concentrated on becoming calmer, forcing myself to relax and concentrate on the lights.

When the red lights go off you want to get off the line as fast as humanly and mechanically possible. This means applying as much power as possible with as little wheelspin as possible. The start can be dangerous because many drivers have the habit of weaving back and forth. They might use the excuse of getting sideways because of too much wheelspin, but you wonder if they aren't trying to block other cars. I believe you should just go straight ahead unless you're moving over to pass someone. With so many cars jockeying for position in the first few metres after the start it can be really hairy, especially if you're back in the pack. Fortunately I've usually started near the front.

Traffic going into the first corner can be very heavy. Problems occur when people try to brake too late or go for the same piece of road that others have chosen. If you're alone in front there is less of a problem, but when there are cars all around, just millimetres away, it's harder to be keep out of trouble. But it's part of your job to avoid hitting people and you have to hope they're also doing their jobs.

Once you're up to speed one of the main tasks is to be able to reduce that speed by braking at exactly the right places. This is best done by using reference points or markers around the track. Before some corners there are marker boards showing the distances to the corner. Other reference points can be advertising billboards, specific points on kerbs, even skid marks on the track that you have memorized. You mustn't use a mobile reference point like a track marshal or flagman – in case they move!

Sometimes, where there are no obvious reference points, you can use past experience to determine where you should brake. It's not as precise as using a marker, but with experience on the circuit you can feel that you've been accelerating long enough and now it's time to start braking. That's the technique

I used in the Eau Rouge section at Spa where so much is going on in a crazy blur of time and space.

Efficient braking is important when you're overtaking another car going into a corner. Basically, the strategy is simply to brake later than your rival. Overtaking can also be achieved by accelerating more quickly coming out of a corner, or pulling out of the slipstream of a car you've been following down a straight, though using a tow to overtake is not easy to do in F1 because the reduced downforce in the wake of another car adversely affects the handling of your car.

When overtaking you have to be very decisive, seizing any opportunity the moment it appears. You can also plan an overtaking move ahead of time, though it becomes harder the longer you stay behind a car because you tend to get into the habit of just following. Also, if you wait too long the other driver becomes more aware of you and the element of surprise can be lost.

To overtake successfully you have to have maximum confidence in your own judgement and also trust the judgement of the other driver.

With experience you get to know what to expect from certain drivers. Even when you're lapping much slower backmarkers you have to be careful they don't do something unexpected, as I found out the hard way a couple of times this season. While some drivers tend to get flustered and make mistakes in close encounters others, like Michael Schumacher, know exactly what they're doing. This is why I had no hesitation in trying to overtake Michael, and when I was able to do it, as in Portugal, it was really rewarding because he is such a good driver.

COMPETITION

Competition is a bit like food for me. It's something I enjoy and need. Not only do I need competition, I need to win or at least believe that I have a chance to win. Nobody likes being beaten, especially if something can be done to prevent it.

Because of the difficulty in overtaking, pit stops are often the best way of improving your position on the track. This is what happened in Portugal, where an efficient stop was a big factor in my winning the race. When it becomes time to make a pit stop the team tells you over the radio and on the signalling board at the pit wall, but it's usually been planned in advance and you're prepared for it.

When you're making a pit stop you try to get in as quickly as possible, including going into the pit entrance, though you have to take care not to exceed the pit lane speed limit. You also brake as late as possible for the pit crew, but you have to stop exactly on the mark. There are a lot of people working on the car and the few seconds you're stationary are pressure-packed. You have to stay very alert so you can make a quick getaway. You keep the car in neutral until the new wheels are on and the fuel is in, and when you get the signal to go you floor it.

Back out on the track you have to deal with both fast and slow corners. On a quick corner you try to keep the car as stable as possible, avoiding abrupt changes of attitude in the chassis. You don't want to brake hard and throw the car sideways.

Everything has to be done smoothly so you can feel exactly what the car is doing. When the car is set up right, you just come off the throttle, brake gently and then feed the throttle back on progressively.

Cornering quickly in this way is one of the best driving pleasures, but if the handling is not right you do whatever you can to drive around the problem. Usually you don't pump the accelerator or brake pedal in a quick corner, but it's sometimes necessary to compensate for a setup deficiency. In this case you tap the brakes or apply a burst of extra power to try and transfer more or less weight over the front or back wheels.

Slower corners, hairpin bends and most chicanes require more abrupt movements from the driver and I find them not nearly as much fun. They force you out of a flowing rhythm and also, because they are slower and more boring, you're deprived of the pleasure of being on the edge. If you go over the edge in a slow corner you may have a spin, and that's it. The thrill of taking a quick corner on the limit is closely related to the element of risk, and slow corners simply don't get your heart pumping.

JAPANESE GRAND PRIX

SUZUKA, JAPAN, 13 OCTOBER 1996

My first F1 season ended in a gravel trap, after a wheel fell off the car. But there was no real despair because overall it had been a positive year. There had been nothing to lose in this race, only something to gain – the championship. While that was lost to my team mate Damon Hill, our achievements over the balance of the season will always be there to savour.

After winning the last race, in Portugal, it was business as usual, testing at the Estoril circuit. That went well as did the following few days, visiting my girlfriend Sandrine in Canada. It was a good way to relax before what would be the most crucial race of the season, from the championship point of view. If I won the race and Damon failed to score points the World Championship would be mine. It was a slim chance, but with the odds so much in his favour I felt there was more pressure on Damon than on me, because it would be a big upset if he was beaten by the underdog.

Because of the championship showdown there was more media attention than ever when we came to Japan. For instance, I was asked how big a disappointment it would be if Damon beat me for the championship.

My answer was that it would be more of a disappointment now that we were closer in the standings. The championship had come down to this final race, but everything that had happened in the previous 15 races had contributed to the situation we were now facing. Both of us had done things to win and lose the championship. But it's the same for any driver, and if you look back over a season there are many things you would do differently. Overall, I explained, I was very pleased to still be in contention, and no matter what happened in the final race of the season I would be happy about the year.

All season long some journalists had been trying to find signs of a personal feud between Damon and me, and now, at the climax of our battle, some were convinced we should hate each other. I was asked what methods I would use to attempt to put extra pressure on Damon.

They were probably disappointed to hear that I don't believe in exerting pressure off the track by playing psychological games with your opponents. I don't think that kind of behaviour is fair. Instead, you should confine your competition to the track and you should keep it clean. And concerning my relationship with Damon, if there was any change it had only been for the better as the season went on. Even here in Japan, with everything on the line, we were laughing and joking together more than ever. There had never been any problem between us, and we had some great battles on the track and lots of fun off it.

You don't have to hate each other to have great battles in racing cars, in fact, that kind of attitude is a wasted effort and it can also be dangerous. As far as doing anything silly in the race, like trying to take Damon off, that would provide absolutely no satisfaction. No matter how badly you want to win, you have to live with yourself afterwards and there would be no glory in winning by using dirty tricks.

Then I was asked if I thought Damon deserved to be champion. Certainly I thought he deserved it. He had been working hard for many years to get to this point in his career, and it's all the work that you put into racing that eventually pays you back. And for the same reason I thought I deserved it too! But if I didn't win my confidence would be intact because the payoff – a championship – would surely come my way in the future.

The journalists wanted to know if this was the biggest race of my career. Yes, there was a lot at stake but there was not much I could do about it. All I could do was run my own race and the rest would depend on Damon.

And if I were a betting man would I bet on myself? You bet I would, because I believe in myself. But every driver has to believe in himself in every race and believing in yourself is more important than ever when the stakes are really high.

"He's a great guy. He puts a lot of emphasis on the relationship between driver and race engineer. The contrast in his personality is quite distinct. There's the maturity he shows in looking after everything he does in his racing. He doesn't miss a trick. Yet when it comes to a sense of humour, enjoying life and just larking around, he's like an overgrown schoolboy at times."

JOCK CLEAR *(Williams race engineer)*

Finally, the journalists wanted to know how I would deal with not winning the championship. This was a hard one to answer because it would involve negative thinking, something I try to avoid. The only thing I could promise was that – win or lose – we would have a good party on Sunday night. It would be better if the party was to celebrate a win, but if not, feeling bad the next day would help take my mind off the loss!

It helped that our championship showdown would be held in the familiar environment of Japan, where I had enjoyed racing in the 1992 Formula 3 series. That had been a good year, and it was a pleasure to renew old acquaintances and to visit the Suzuka circuit again. This is one of the few real road racing circuits that remain and I was eager to find out what it would be like in an F1 car. From the beginning of the race weekend the track lived up to expectations, and even though it was wet during most of practice the car felt very good.

The circuit is wonderfully satisfying because its sequence of high and medium speed corners are arranged so that they flow together and you can really get into a good rhythm. The lap is spoiled somewhat by a silly slow chicane, but that also adds to the complexity and when everything works out – the car setup is exactly right and the driver gets everything right – Suzuka gives you a terrific sense of accomplishment, similar to the way it is at Spa in Belgium. After you really attack a lap – throwing everything you have into Suzuka's 5.864 kilometres so that you're right on the edge all the way round – you feel really complete as a driver.

Certainly, it felt that way in qualifying. One of the most difficult corners is called 130-R, and being able to take it flat out at over 300 kilometres per hour helped produce the lap that gave me pole position. But this was only a preliminary victory in the real battle, which would take place in the race. On Sunday morning I took longer than usual to prepare for that battle, thinking about what I had to do as, for the final time in the season, I followed the ritual of getting into my racing gear.

The first thing I had to do was insert the contact lenses I wear when I drive. Out of the car I wear glasses, but contacts don't move around as much and they won't fog up inside the helmet. I also wear moulded ear plugs but even with them I think F1 engines are loud enough to cause hearing damage. If I forget my earplugs when I go out to a disco where loud music is being played I stuff tissue in my ears. People may look at me as if I'm an idiot but I insist on taking care of my ears.

In racing I also believe in taking care of my head, so a lot of time is spent looking after my helmet. By the time we got to Japan I had probably gone through a dozen of them in the season. You have to change them frequently because the foam expands from all the sweating, and a helmet has to be thrown away after a crash in case it has been damaged. In each race you go through about five tear-off strips, the strips of clear plastic that cover the visor, throwing them away as they become dirty with oil and dust. When a helmet becomes too dirty and pitted from oil and flying stone chips, it's also time to throw it away because any extra layers of fresh paint would add more weight.

Under the helmet I keep the fireproof balaclava away from my nose and mouth. Most drivers only have openings for their eyes. I don't know how they do it. I prefer getting all the fresh air I can. I also wear a full set of fireproof underwear that includes a turtleneck top, instead of just the T-shirt some drivers wear, and after I wear them once I change my socks because sweaty socks would be worse in a fire. Before getting into the car I take off my watch, and wear no jewellery because metal will heat up more quickly in a fire and cause burns.

Getting rid of accessories also saves some weight, even if it is only a few grams, which helps because the driving suit is fairly heavy. In the car the sponsors' logos on the arms can be irritating because they are hard patches that curtail freedom. In the cockpit the slightest bulge in your clothing can bunch up and bug you. My suits are deliberately oversized and have no pockets or belts. I don't care if I look like a potato sack as long as it feels good in the car. By the time I had fastened my driving

shoes and pulled on my gloves we were ready to begin the
Japanese Grand Prix.

With Damon second on the grid the final fight between the
world championship contenders would begin on the front row.
This added to the drama for the spectators and increased the
importance of the start for the drivers. Unfortunately, my
worst start of the season came in the most important race.

When the red lights went out, I failed to apply enough
throttle and the engine revs dropped. To compensate for
getting bogged down I then applied too much power and got a
huge amount of wheelspin. The car went sideways, and by the
time I got it all sorted out five people had passed me, led by
Damon who had made a perfect start.

This was a huge setback for my championship hopes, but the
goal remained the same. There was no option but to try
everything possible to somehow win the race and hope that
Damon would fail to finish in the points. That was the
background philosophy, but in reality all thoughts of the
championship were set aside and my concentration was
focussed completely on driving as hard as I possibly could – just
like in qualifying.

And while it lasted, the rest of my race was great fun –
mainly because I was able to pass other cars. It was very
satisfying to be able to do this and to confirm again that
overtaking in F1 is feasible if you try hard enough. Of course
you need a good car, and at this point mine was running
perfectly, setting lap times quicker than anybody else,
including the fastest lap of the race. Shortly after that our
Japanese Grand Prix was over.

Just before our second pit stop the rear of the car began

moving strangely, the way it might if a tyre was punctured. Under braking for the pit entrance the car twitched alarmingly and I had to make another full lap before coming in for fuel and fresh tyres. After the pit stop everything felt fine again, but the feeling of security only lasted a few more laps.

Suddenly, in the middle of Suzuka's first corner, the left front wheel rose up in the air, which suggested something was seriously wrong on the right side at the rear of the car. This theory was confirmed when the right rear wheel overtook me at about 250 kilometres per hour!

The car slewed sideways and then slid straight off the circuit into a gravel trap. But the flying wheel kept on going, and it was a relief to find out later that the fences prevented it from hitting anyone in the crowd. We found out later that the wheel came off because some retaining pins failed to keep a wheel nut in place. There was no point in blaming anyone, it was just a racing incident, the kind of thing that is bound to happen occasionally.

On the long walk back to the pits the generous applause of the spectators helped ease some of the disappointment at having the race, and the season, end on a negative note. But at least we had put on a good show, fighting hard all the way – from the first lap in Australia until the last lap in Japan.

At the end of the race I joined the rest of the team along the pit wall and cheered Damon home. He drove a perfect race and deserved to win and I was pleased for him. Above all, he had a great season and deserved to be World Champion. He was also an excellent team mate and we were both fortunate in having the best people on our side. Everyone at Williams worked hard for our success and it had been a pleasure to reward all their effort with a strong showing. I was especially grateful to all the guys who worked on my car, and my race engineer Jock Clear deserved special thanks.

In fact, I was so grateful to Jock that after the race I helped put him out of the misery he suffered from losing the bet we made earlier in the season. To pay his debt he had to have his head shaved in Japan. This made poor Jock look so ridiculous that I had my head shaved in sympathy. Misery loves company so I persuaded David Coulthard and Mika Salo that having their heads shaved might make them faster!

Then we went to a big party where everyone sang and had a good time, including the bald-headed quartet. Even Damon and Michael Schumacher (who finished third in the championship) joined in the fun. Win or lose, we all had something to celebrate. In my case, it was a most satisfactory conclusion to my first F1 season.

" Jacques has amazed us this year. Who would have thought last March that a complete F1 rookie would be in a position to challenge for the drivers' title just eight months on? For his first season he has put in a remarkable showing. And we have certainly yet to see his best, for he has many seasons in F1 ahead of him."

PATRICK FAURE *(President, Renault Sport)*

" I think Damon had a little bit more speed at first, but Jacques got stronger as the year went on. Jacques stepped his game up, but he needed to. In the middle of the year he was looking a bit dodgy. But he's mentally very strong, very confident, very aggressive. He is very tough, a good little racer - and he had a Williams to work with."

EDDIE IRVINE *(Ferrari driver)*

Rearview Mirror

L ooking back at my first season in F1 racing the memories are mainly positive. Though I had a few ideas of what the experience would be like I never tell myself how things are going to be because they often turn out differently than you expect. Being with a great team and having a great car made us always in contention for a win or a podium finish. From the advantage of that perspective it's hard to find anything negative.

It was tough in the beginning because I had so much to learn. It was easier in Australia because the Melbourne track was new to everybody but in most of the following races I had to learn the tracks while also learning about F1. Playing catchup all the time was sometimes difficult and discouraging. But eventually we got our bearings and improved the car and things progressed fairly steadily.

It was a bit disappointing to find so many of the tracks modernized and deprived of the character and challenges you relish as a driver. It's good to have a variety of different circuits but when you race at super places like Suzuka and Spa you realize what you're missing in the others.

The season seemed to go slowly because so much effort was packed into it. The races went quickly enough but with all the testing and PR work between the races there was no time to sit down and think. There were only a few short breaks and mostly it felt like eight months of heavy work. In the end it was tiring, both mentally and physically.

There was a lot of pressure to deal with, not so much from others but from myself because their expectations for my first season weren't as high as mine. The self-induced pressure was to always do my best and to continue to improve. From that point of view I'm happy with what I accomplished. Winning a quarter of the races, starting from the front row in over half of them and scoring points in 11 of the 16 races was good from a results point of view. Every points-scoring finish was on the podium and the fact that the last half of the season was better than the first showed that the improvement was there. Even the mistakes made in the races, either by myself or others, were not a complete waste because the lessons learned can only help in the future.

The best moments that come immediately to mind were the pole positions, in Australia, Belgium and Japan. Those are the three best circuits so there must be some connection to doing well on them. Of course, all the wins were great and the best of them was in Portugal, not just because of the win which was crucial to keep the championship alive but because of the way it was won, by making overtaking moves and driving really hard.

Among the best memories are the close fights with other drivers. The best of them during the season were with Damon and Michael Schumacher and being able to overtake them, and others, on occasion were real highlights for me. It is also satisfying to remember that I never stopped fighting in any of the races.

I would prefer to forget the worst moments – losing in Australia after coming so close to winning, making a stupid mistake in the rain in Brazil, the pain in the posterior that was Monaco, the pain in the neck from the accident in France, coming second in my home race in Canada, making an even more stupid mistake in Italy, a race where I could have really closed the gap to Damon. The mistakes are the most aggravating memory because without them the championship could have been mine. Last season in IndyCar racing I never threw away points through my own mistakes. But I will never find excuses or mourn over the lost opportunities.

Losing the championship in the last race of the season in Japan quickly faded from a bad memory to just a disappointment. It was easier to accept because Damon had been such strong opposition throughout the season. Finishing second to a worthy World Champion can't be all that bad.

A lot of the credit for our success has to go to the Rothmans Williams Renault team. The cars you see on the track are really only the tip of the iceberg and everybody in the team made a contribution. Next season we will all be one year better and there is every reason to expect improvement. The objectives will be the same – to win as many races as possible and the world championship – and we should have an even better chance of achieving them.

" We took a stab in the dark with Jacques, but it paid off. I do like to see the car have its neck wrung and he certainly does that."

PATRICK HEAD *(Williams Technical Director)*

" Jacques had a truly remarkable season. As a newcomer he had a lot of work to do and he did it exceedingly well. To be in contention for the championship throughout the season is the highest possible praise. Well done, Jacques."

FRANK WILLIAMS *(Williams team owner)*

" Jacques was a match for me by the end of the season, but my motivation was to keep ahead and win the championship. He was coming from behind and could take more risks. I am the first to appreciate that fate could have stepped in and Jacques could have finished the season as champion. When he first came to the team I didn't know what to think, but quickly reached the conclusion that he's a very fine racing driver. I've enjoyed being with Jacques - there has not been a harsh word between us. I have no doubt that he will be a world champion of the future. It's an experience I can strongly recommend."

DAMON HILL *(1996 World Champion)*

Between seasons

ONE SEASON ENDS...

O ur big party at the Suzuka circuit after the Japanese Grand Prix was an important occasion, not just because it provided a chance to celebrate the end of my first season in F1. It had been a memorable year, with plenty of good hard racing, some respectable results and many new experiences, but it had also been packed with pressure and tension, both on and off the track. So it was a welcome relief to finally be able to release inhibitions and relax.

Being an F1 driver is one of the greatest jobs in the world but it's not all fun and games. In fact, a Grand Prix season is mostly very hard work, even for veteran drivers, and because a newcomer has to learn on the job he has even more to do. In my case there had been nearly two years of solid effort, with hardly any opportunity to completely cut away from it all since the beginning of the 1995 IndyCar season. I put everything I had into my racing and it paid off, but winning the IndyCar Championship and finishing second in the 1996 F1 World Drivers' Championship had taken a mental and physical toll that left me very much in need of a real holiday.

The morning after our party at Suzuka, Mika Salo and I went to Tokyo, where we had become friends when we raced in

Japan a few years ago. Tokyo is such a big city that you can usually walk around without attracting much attention but this time it was a bit different. At first we thought people were staring at us because we were famous racing drivers. Then we realised it was probably our bald heads that made us the focus of so much interest! We had a fun couple of days, visiting the places where we used to live, renewing old acquaintances and re-living some good memories from a time when racing wasn't so serious.

From Tokyo I flew back to Canada to see Sandrine. By then I had almost forgotten about my lack of hair but she quickly reminded me of it. At first she was worried that I might be sick, because my shaved head was white and she thought it made me look pale and anaemic. But she soon decided that I wasn't unwell – just crazy! At least it was cold in Montreal and most of the time I had to wear a hat. We spent some time visiting relatives and friends, had a couple of parties, and generally relaxed, had fun and enjoyed ourselves. It was a welcome treat to just be normal again and be happy and not have a care in the world.

Back home in Monaco the holiday mood continued. I spent many hours reading and listening to music, and managed to reduce the pile of books and CDs that had accumulated over the season, played computer games and went out with friends for drinks and meals. A group of us got together for one of my favourite pastimes, a marathon session of the role-playing game, 'Dungeons and Dragons'. It went on for about 16 hours and in that time I only took about five minutes off. This game is not only great fun but it also requires your complete attention, and the intense concentration helps keep your mind in trim.

While all the recreational activities kept me busy my body was having a well-earned rest. After a couple of weeks without much strenuous physical activity it was easier to start training again, to prepare to go back to work.

One of the first obligations was to make a presentation to the winners of the Best Rock Act at the MTV Music Awards in London. This was a lot of fun (not just because I had to work with the beautiful supermodel Helena Christensen!) and the award went to 'The Smashing Pumpkins', a band I like very much.

Next on the agenda was a two-day test session at the Paul Ricard circuit followed by four days at Estoril. After having been out of the car for over a month I found the first day a bit tiring, but after that there was no problem. We completed 90 laps on that opening day, and before we packed up we had completed a distance equivalent to several Grands Prix. I was in much better shape and more relaxed compared to last year at this time, when I was tired from doing so much testing without a break.

The main purpose of these tests was to try out the new Renault engine, and even though Renault had plans to leave F1 at the end of the 1997 season it was obvious they were as serious as ever about racing. Compared to the RS8, the new RS9 engine was smaller and lighter and it revved higher and had more power at the top end. But I thought the biggest gain would come from its lower centre of gravity which should improve the car's handling.

Until the new car was ready we used an interim chassis. The Williams FW18B was essentially the 1996 car with the RS9 engine. Our new car, the FW19, looked very promising on paper and even though there were no big visual differences it would be very different mechanically. I was quite optimistic about it, partly because the new design incorporated some of my thinking. The FW19 would be an evolution of a winning car so there was every reason to believe it should be an improvement; and with our experience from last year we had the basic setup points to work from, so we expected the development of the FW19 to progress quickly.

"Jacques has the experience. He knows the team and the people. He knows the car very well and he's very sharp. He's also very motivated and very clever. He will go for it."
HEINZ-HARALD FRENTZEN (Williams driver)

Early in December we went to South Africa on a promotional trip for our sponsors. We did a few demonstration laps around the Kyalami circuit and I was amazed to see the grandstands packed with a huge crowd of F1 fans. Obviously, the South Africans are very keen to have a Grand Prix again, though it would be hard to fit another race into the crowded schedule we have now. With 17 races in 1997, we would be busier than ever.

The post-season activities at the circuits gave me a chance to get to know my new team-mate better. I first met Heinz-Harald Frentzen when we both raced in Japan, where our careers overlapped for a couple of months, and more recently we had seen each other from time to time in Monaco, where he also lives. Heinz is a friendly guy and seemed easy to get along with, which is important when you have to work together, and he is obviously a quick driver. I had a healthy respect for him and knew that the team would give us completely equal equipment and that I would have to work hard in what was sure to be a keen rivalry.

During the 1996 season, Damon Hill and I had the best kind of rivalry that team-mates can have. On the track we were fierce competitors and fought hard but we always respected each other. Off the track we were friendly, and this is much more enjoyable for everyone concerned. It's also more productive because if team-mates become enemies, it can undermine team spirit and interfere with progress and success.

One of the best things about F1 for me so far, besides the racing, had been the positive relationships that developed with some of the drivers. As a newcomer I was pleased to see that you can race against people and still enjoy their company socially. It's important that you can do this once in a while, competing with them and then sharing a laugh with them later. This was the way it was in IndyCar racing where some of us brought our own motorhomes to the tracks and in the evenings we visited each other often. In F1 we all stay in hotel rooms, but it was good to see that even here you can also get along well with your rivals if you're willing to try. Besides forming close friendships with Mika Salo and David Coulthard, I also had a good relationship with Damon, and with Michael Schumacher. For sure, Michael is one of the hardest racers, and we had some great battles, but we also managed to have a few laughs together and developed a mutual respect that is very important when you're operating at close quarters on the track.

Good relationships are vital when it comes to teamwork and that played a big part in what Williams accomplished in 1996. Naturally, I was closest to Jock Clear and the guys who worked on my car; but all the other relationships were entirely positive, including those with our bosses. It helps that we all share a racing mentality. Patrick Head wasn't at every Grand Prix but when he came he really got into it. You only had to see him jumping around in the pits for proof of that. Patrick is a great guy and so is Frank. You can see that he eats, sleeps and breathes racing. He's not only a team owner but he's a racer at heart and that's inspirational for us all. Everyone at Williams was going to have to follow his example if our success was to continue in 1997.

In the coming season the pressure from other teams was bound to be more intense. When you are on top, as Williams were in 1996, everybody works harder to beat you and the better your car is, the more difficult it is to find room for improvement, so we fully expected some of the other teams would have a good chance of getting closer to us. This would be good for the fans as well as the drivers, because we all thrive on competition.

If you raced with a car that was two seconds a lap quicker than the others because of its mechanical superiority (which has never happened to me!) it would be very boring. You would be alone out in front without competition, you wouldn't have to go to the edge and there wouldn't be much point in racing. Everybody wants to win but the real pleasure, the sense of accomplishment, comes from having to fight for what you get, and there was bound to be plenty of that in the coming season.

Many people were suggesting I should be the favourite to

win the Championship. It was natural to think this way because the circumstances and the momentum should be in my favour. I was second in the 1996 Driver's Championship, after improving steadily throughout the season; I was staying with a winning team where the chemistry among the personnel should be stronger than ever; and with one year's experience in F1 racing things should go even better for me. All of this was valid, but in my mind I knew it wasn't going to be that easy and I expected my second season would be similar to the first: a battle from start to finish.

Before getting more serious about the coming season we had some time off at the end of the year, which reminded me to start thinking about buying Christmas presents. Christmas is a family time and ours would be spent with my mother and little sister at our country home up in the mountains behind Monaco. We've had our chalet for a long time and it was here, when I was very young, that I first learned to ski.

Before Christmas David Coulthard and I were invited to have some fun in Mika Salo's native land. Mika had arranged for us to go snowmobiling in northern Finland and as it turned out David had a previous engagement and couldn't make the trip, so he missed all the action. Mika and I had a blast, roaring around through the snow for hours on end, even though there is very little daylight in that part of the world at this time of year. After the second day I felt like a robot that was out of oil. Every inch of my body was hurting, because different muscles are used when you're controlling a bouncing snowmobile. It was a huge workout, and good for my training. It was also very cold but that's nothing new for a Canadian, though it helped that our hair was growing back to help keep us warm!

We celebrated New Year's Eve with more winter sport, in Switzerland, where Mika, David and I rented a big chalet. There were about 20 people in our international group, including our girlfriends. Mika's girlfriend Noriko is from Japan and gets along well with Andrea, David's girlfriend, and Sandrine, who are both Canadians. There was lots of snow in the Alps so the skiing was great and so was the company. We tried, but failed, to get David to wear his Scottish kilt so we could see him dancing in it! Anyway, it was a Happy New Year for all of us.

That was the fun side of the end of the year and, too soon, it seemed, we would have to apply ourselves to the serious business of getting ourselves and our cars into gear to go racing again. From about the middle of January we would be testing almost non-stop until the first race in March. I was enthusiastic about this because the preparations for my second F1 season would be purely developing the car, bringing it up to speed instead of myself, and by the time we got to Australia we expected to be in good shape. I was really looking forward to it.

ANOTHER SEASON BEGINS...

Like everyone else in F1, our team spent the early part of 1997 preparing for the new season. It's an anxious time of year because so much depends on the new equipment you have to work with and no matter how good everything looks on paper, you're never sure about the car until you actually drive it. In our case it was a pleasure to find out that our car peformed as good as it looked. The mechanical package we had to work with seemed a major step forward from last year. It would have to be because, as the old saying goes, to stand still in F1 is to go backward.

Our new FW19 chassis was immediately quick in testing and it responded well to set-up changes which is important when it comes to making the constant progress you need to keep pace throughout the season. The chassis was designed to accommodate the new Renault RS9 engine and it, too, was performing well. As we expected, the lighter and lower engine helped improve the car's handling, which was already quite good. The thing I liked best about the new car was that it was more predictable, meaning I could push it to the limit without being surprised by its reactions. It was also reassuringly reliable and on our final day of pre-season testing I completed 140 quick laps with no problems. All in all, we were confident that we had the equipment to successfully defend the Championships, both the team and driving titles, that Williams won last year.

Morale in the team was high and my new team-mate was settling in well. Heinz-Harald was always smiling, which was a good sign. Though we take our racing very seriously the Williams team is also noted for having a good sense of humour and having fun while you work hard is the best way to go racing.

Personally, having enjoyed some time off to relax and recharge my batteries, I never felt better about approaching a new season. The workload over the past few months had been a lot easier than last year because by the time we got to the first Grand Prix of 1996 we had done over 10,000 kilometres of testing and it was inevitable that there was a certain amount of fatigue. There was also some apprehension – about settling into a new team, having to learn so many new tracks, finding out how the other drivers would behave in racing conditions, fulfilling all the media and public relations obligations and generally coming to grips with the complicated business of being an F1 driver.

"It's going to be interesting between the Williams drivers. Frentzen is fast and he may do quite a good job in qualifying. But Jacques is a good, intelligent racer. Frentzen's got some stuff to learn about being in front and the additional pressures that he's going to be under driving for a front-running team, whereas Jacques is already up to speed on that. It may be close but I would give Jacques the edge."

DAMON HILL
(Arrows driver and reigning World Champion)

This year there would be fewer unknown factors and the job now was to build on what had been a successful debut season. Following our good performances in pre-season testing, the prediction that I would become the 1997 World Champion was now more widespread. Of course, this brought extra pressure but it was a positive kind of pressure because, unlike last year, they were not expecting me to fall flat on my face!

Instead of having to prove people wrong, I would have to prove them right, which somehow seemed easier. Living up to all the expectations, my own as well as those of others, should also be easier because of the extra confidence gained from having done well in 1996. Every driver has to believe in himself, but some doubts remain until you've actually proven that you're capable of winning.

Another thing you have to remember is that there are very few certainties in racing, beyond the fact that winning is never easy. Based on what we had seen in pre-season testing, winning would be harder than ever in 1997 because all the top teams had obviously improved. We expected the strongest opposition to come from Benetton, McLaren and Ferrari, while the impressive testing times set by the Ligier team (which later changed its name to Prost Grand Prix) on Bridgestone tyres suggested that those of us on Goodyears would have a tyre war on our hands. Having a second tyre manufacturer in F1 would add another dimension to the competition, and also an element of unpredictability that could have an effect on the results.

To get the best results my plan was to drive aggressively in the early races, continuing the momentum that developed over the second half of the 1996 season, to try and build up a points advantage as quickly as possible. The theory was that by doing well in the first races, while the opposition was still finding its way, you would avoid having to play catch-up and that would be crucial to achieving our ultimate goal: winning the Championship.

This strategy was slightly different than last year, when the objective was first of all to try to be competitive and if that was possible then we would try to win some races and over the season collect enough points to be in contention for the Championship. That's the way it turned out, but this year we were beginning from a position of greater strength and the intention was to hit the ground running, get in front and stay there. Of course, other drivers had the same idea – that's what competition is all about – and that's why we go racing.

From nowhere to back in front

NOWHERE IN AUSTRALIA...

My first race of the 1997 season lasted only 300 metres. To describe my Australian Grand Prix as a huge disappointment would be an understatement; in fact, when my car ended up in a gravel trap a few seconds after the start of the race, I used some words that must not appear in this book!

Our trip to Melbourne started on a positive note with a short break in Miami, where the first race of the IndyCar season was being held. The name of the series had been changed to CART (Championship Auto Racing Teams) but the atmosphere, which I remember fondly, seemed unchanged from my two seasons in this category of racing. It was a pleasant change to become immersed in that world again, meeting some of the guys I used to compete against and spending some time with the people on my old IndyCar team. I have to admit that sometimes I miss driving on an oval track, which is quite unlike anything we have in F1. Being in this environment again was a reminder of the different race tactics and, above all, the terrific sensation of exhilaration you get when you're driving at very high speeds very close to the cement walls.

My stopover in Miami was also an opportunity to visit some

old school friends from Switzerland who now live in America. One of them is a computer programmer and as you might expect when two computer addicts get together there is only one thing on the agenda. We spent an entire evening shopping for computers and talking about them before it was time to continue the long trip to Australia.

I arrived in Melbourne, fresh, relaxed and motivated. Although the start of the new season meant a return to all the pressures of F1, at least I knew what to expect, and how to handle it better. Being with the same team and having worked steadily in testing over the winter break made getting back into the race routine that much easier. It helped that I liked the Albert Park circuit and having made a successful F1 debut there last year, with pole position and a strong second place finish, gave me extra confidence. Everything was comfortably familiar, though there would be at least one major difference, because of the competition between the two tyre manufacturers.

Both Goodyear and Bridgestone offer their teams a choice of two rubber compounds, a harder one which has less grip but lasts longer and a softer one which gives better grip but doesn't wear as well. During the two hours of practice on Friday each team has to choose its tyres for the weekend and this requires more work, evaluating tyre performance and planning race strategy that varies, depending on the choice of tyre. With a limit of 30 practice laps on Friday you use up a lot of time that last year was spent working on the car setup.

At least I didn't have to waste time learning the circuit and it felt great to be back in the cockpit for some real action on Friday. Right away we found that the car was competitive compared to the opposition on either tyre compound, and by the end of the day we had decided to go with the softer version of Goodyear tyres. That night I went to bed fairly happy, confident that we were looking good for the rest of the weekend.

"With a year's experience behind us, Jacques and I think that we're going to be working better together, that we'll be more quickly up to speed at all the circuits now that he knows them better, and generally we expect to perform better than we did in 1996. Since we were runners-up last year we can only expect to do better this year. Our aspiration is to win the World Championship and we'll be very disappointed if we don't achieve it."

JOCK CLEAR *(Williams race engineer)*

By the time the engines were shut off on Saturday we were in the best possible position: on pole for the race. The fourth pole lap of my F1 career wasn't exactly perfect – when you're trying that hard you usually make small mistakes – but it was quicker than anyone else by a considerable margin. Some of the extra speed came from the confidence of having a great car that was very driveable right on the edge of adhesion, and sometimes a bit beyond it! You could really lean on it – get it sideways, yet still catch it – which is a terrific feeling.

The only problem we had before the race was extra wear on

the brakes, caused by the better grip of the softer tyres, which meant the brakes were getting spongy after a few laps. Overnight, my engineer Jock Clear and the guys who work on the car made some changes and we felt everything was ready to go for 58 laps around the Albert Park circuit. The full race distance would be around 306 kilometres but I was destined to travel only a tiny fraction of that.

Knowing that we had a very good car it was important to use it to best advantage from the very beginning. Being a second and a half quicker than anybody else in qualifying is useless if you don't start well. I would describe my start as average, although the clutch slipped a bit just as we left the line. My team-mate Heinz-Harald Frentzen took the lead and I was in second place with Eddie Irvine's Ferrari coming up on my right and Johnny Herbert's Sauber on the left. We were all fighting for position and it was going fairly smoothly until we got into the first turn, where Irvine, who was on the inside where the track surface was dirty and there was less grip, braked later than anybody else. Suddenly there were three cars in a corner which barely has room for two. Herbert and I were squeezed off the track and out of the race and Irvine, whose car had made contact with mine in the incident, also had to stop.

You have to take chances in racing. Irvine took a chance that didn't work and his mistake cost the three of us dearly. For me, it was an extremely exasperating conclusion to a race that had promised so much. We knew we had the quickest car in Australia but having the quickest car in the world means absolutely nothing when it's parked in a gravel trap. Irvine and I had to wait until the end of the race to meet the Stewards to explain what happened. Unfortunately, nobody wanted to take the blame, nor apportion it, which irritated me even more.

The Australian Grand Prix was won by David Coulthard in his McLaren. David was always at the top of my list of serious opponents for the 1997 Championship and I was happy for him. So was the third member of our trio, Mika Salo (whose Tyrrell didn't finish the race), and we went out together on Sunday evening in Melbourne. Helping a friend celebrate his victory was a good way to avoid dwelling on the negative outcome of the first race of the season.

The early races are always the most important ones. Your main objective is to score as many points as possible. If you don't do it at the start, you have to play catch-up and that's the position the whole team was in, because Heinz-Harald had been forced out of the race with a brake problem. Our only consolation was that there were still 16 races to go. Now, we would have to forget about our non-event in Australia and consider the next race, in Brazil, as the start of our season.

BACK IN FRONT IN BRAZIL...

It came one race later than it should have but that made winning the Brazilian Grand Prix all the better. We put all our problems behind us, gathered ourselves together for a maximum effort and came away from the weekend in Sao Paulo with pole position, fastest race lap and a victory that put us back on track for the championship.

Besides the personal pleasure of conquering the Interlagos circuit, one that I don't really like, it was very satisfying to finally lead the team into the forefront, where we all think we should be, and to show that we have what it takes to stay there.

Most of the interval between the first two races of the season was spent travelling considerable distances, both in my racing car and, less successfully, in commercial aircraft. One of the reasons I don't like flying is that you have less control over your own destiny and our complicated and very tedious journey out of Australia made that feeling stronger than ever.

I wanted to leave Australia as quickly as possible, to forget about the race but mainly to see my girfriend and my relatives, in Canada. But it was not an easy journey. I was on a flight with my manager, Craig Pollock, which had to make an emergency landing in Tahiti. This is not a bad place to go for a holiday if that is your objective, but being stuck there for a whole day in the airport was not a fun occasion. When we finally got to Montreal I was very tired and the time I was able to spend with Sandrine and my family was all too short because I had to depart for a test session in France.

At least our testing at the Paul Ricard circuit near Marseilles went according to schedule. Working to improve my starts was a priority and we made useful progress in that department. Likewise, both Heinz-Harald and I were able to successfully complete simulated race distances to test the reliability of the brake modifications we made after our problems in Australia. From Paul Ricard I made the short journey back home to Monaco, where I had only a brief opportunity to unpack my bags before it was time to hit the road again.

En route to Brazil I stopped over in London where 'James', one of my favourite rock groups was performing. I went to the concert with some good friends and later that evening we went out on the town and had a blast. Following that welcome stopover it was time to head for South America, where I would spend the next three weeks.

To become acclimatised to the heat and humidity I went to the Brazilian coast for a few days. I jogged every day on the beach and worked on my conditioning to prepare for one of the most physically demanding races of the season. Two things set Interlagos apart from other circuits: the surface is extremely bumpy and the lap runs counter-clockwise, so most of the turns are to the left. This puts extra strain on your neck muscles, which are more accustomed to withstanding the g-forces of right-hand turns. Interlagos packs a lot of distance into a small space so that it twists around on itself several times which makes it's hard to get a rhythm going. It's one of my least favourite places so it was a bit of a surprise to find everything going smoothly from the beginning of the Grand Prix weekend.

On Friday the car felt strong and handled the bumps quite well. It was also quick and my lap times were faster than I usually do in practice, when the emphasis is on experimenting to find the best setup. On Saturday we made a few changes that improved the handling even more and my first two quick laps in qualifying were good enough for pole position. There was still some time left in the session but my car developed a small radiator leak and I had to jump into the spare car, which was set up this weekend for Heinz-Harald. Jock Clear and the mechanics quickly converted it to suit me, which was good training for them should we have such an emergency in the future. But as it turned out nobody could beat my earlier times and we were in good shape.

As we lined up on the grid to begin the race, I was very

confident but also conscious of the need to make the best of my pole position with a quick start. I managed to do this but so did Michael Schumacher, who was also on the front row, and heading into the first turn his Ferrari was alongside me. I knew my car was faster (in qualifying I beat him by over half a second) and I was determined to stay in front. That was a bad decision because I was on the outside of the track, off the racing line where there is less grip, and the only way I could keep up the momentum through the first turn was by taking a shortcut across the grass and through the gravel. A shower of gravel landed in the cockpit and by the time I got back on course there were some stones under my seat, which was was very uncomfortable and could also be dangerously distracting over the full race distance. Fortunately, I only had to travel a short way before we were shown the red flag. A car had stalled on the grid and was parked in a dangerous position so the race would have to be re-started.

The second start went well for the first few metres, until Michael made another appearance beside me. This time I didn't try to fight him off because I was now confident I could overtake him quickly. I knew he was running with extra downforce, which would slow him down on the straights, and I could also take advantage of the better grip from the new set of tyres we had mounted after my previous off-course excursion.

By the end of the first lap I was in the lead, but it certainly wasn't a straightforward job to stay in front. We had chosen to race with the harder tyre compound but the temperature was cooler than expected so there was even less grip and the car was jumping around uncomfortably over the bumps. Things improved after our first pit stop for a fresh set of tyres, and it was a bit easier to maintain the gap over Gerhard Berger, whose Benetton gave us the strongest opposition during the afternoon. But more cars than usual were clocking competitive lap times which made overtaking on such a tight circuit very difficult.

Keeping the lead required continual concentration and hard work, which became even harder after our final pit stop when, for some reason, the car was very difficult to handle on the last set of tyres. For the remaining 20 laps the chassis was vibrating badly and with 10 laps to go the engine seemed to lose some of its performance. I was really worried because Berger was applying ever more pressure and I must say it was a relief to cross the finish line as the winner of the Brazilian Grand Prix.

It felt really good to be up on the top step of the podium again, to hear the Canadian national anthem being played and to score ten valuable points in both the Constructors' and Driver's Championships. But this victory, my fifth in F1, was one that I would not keep just for the team and myself. The day after the race was Sandrine's birthday and, though she wasn't with me in Brazil, in my mind I was sharing my first win of 1997 with her.

Race Results

THE AUSTRALIAN GRAND PRIX
March 10, 1996

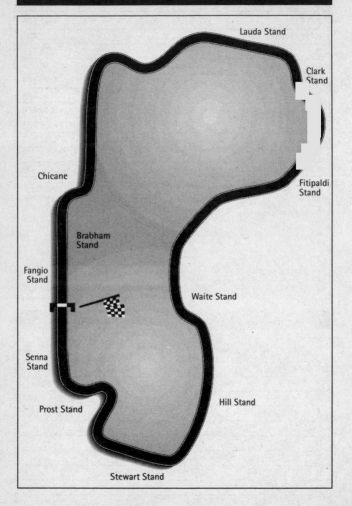

Lauda Stand

Clark
Stand

Chicane

Fitipaldi
Stand

Brabham
Stand

Fangio
Stand

Waite Stand

Senna
Stand

Prost Stand

Hill Stand

Stewart Stand

Qualifying Times

POS	DRIVER	ENTRANT	TIME
1	VILLENEUVE	Williams Renault	1:32.371
2	HILL	Williams Renault	1:32.509
3	IRVINE	Ferrari	1:32.889
4	SCHUMACHER	Ferrari	1:33.125
5	HAKKINEN	McLaren Mercedes	1:34.054
6	ALESI	Benetton Renault	1:34.257
7	BERGER	Benetton Renault	1:34.344
8	BARRICHELLO	Jordan Peugeot	1:34.474
9	FRENTZEN	Sauber Ford	1:34.494
10	SALO	Tyrrell Yamaha	1:34.832
11	PANIS	Ligier Mugen Honda	1:35.330
12	VERSTAPPEN	Footwork Hart	1:35.338
13	COULTHARD	McLaren Mercedes	1:35.351
14	HERBERT	Sauber Ford	1:35.453
15	KATAYAMA	Tyrrell Yamaha	1:35.715
16	FISICHELLA	Minardi Ford	1:35.898
17	LAMY	Minardi Ford	1:36.109
18	ROSSET	Footwork Hart	1:36.198
19	BRUNDLE	Jordan Peugeot	1:36.286
20	DINIZ	Ligier Mugen Honda	1:36.298

Race Results

POS	DRIVER	LAPS	GAP	TIME
1	HILL	58		1:32:50.491
2	VILLENEUVE	58		1:33:28.511
3	IRVINE	58		1:33:53.062
4	BERGER	58		1:34:7.528
5	HAKKINEN	58		1:34:25.562
6	SALO	57	1 lap	
7	PANIS	57	1 lap	
8	FRENTZEN	57	1 lap	
9	ROSSET	56	2 laps	
10	DINIZ	56	2 laps	
11	KATAYAMA	55	3 laps	

Constructors' Points

CONSTRUCTOR	RACE PTS
Williams Renault	16
Ferrari	4
Benetton Renault	3
McLaren Mercedes	2
Tyrrell Yamaha	1

Drivers' Points

DRIVER	RACE PTS
HILL	10
VILLENEUVE	6
IRVINE	4
BERGER	3
HAKKINEN	2
SALO	1

Best Times

Winner's Speed:	Damon Hill		198.736 kph
Fastest Lap:	Jacques Villeneuve	1:33.421	204.313 kph

THE BRAZILIAN GRAND PRIX
March 31, 1996

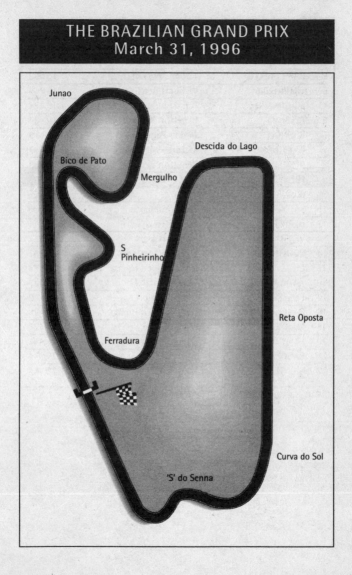

Junao

Descida do Lago

Bico de Pato

Mergulho

S
Pinheirinho

Reta Oposta

Ferradura

Curva do Sol

'S' do Senna

Qualifying Times

POS	DRIVER	ENTRANT	TIME
1	HILL	Williams Renault	1:18.111
2	BARRICHELLO	Jordan Peugeot	1:19.092
3	VILLENEUVE	Williams Renault	1:19.254
4	SCHUMACHER	Ferrari	1:19.474
5	ALESI	Benetton Renault	1:19.484
6	BRUNDLE	Jordan Peugeot	1:19.519
7	HAKKINEN	McLaren Mercedes	1:19.607
8	BERGER	Benetton Renault	1:19.762
9	FRENTZEN	Sauber Ford	1:19.799
10	IRVINE	Ferrari	1:19.951
11	SALO	Tyrrell Yamaha	1:20.000
12	HERBERT	Sauber Ford	1:20.144
13	VERSTAPPEN	Footwork Hart	1:20.157
14	COULTHARD	McLaren Mercedes	1:20.167
15	DINIZ	Ligier Mugen Honda	1:20.873
16	KATAYAMA	Tyrrell Yamaha	1:20.427
17	ROSSET	Footwork Hart	1:20.440
18	PANIS	Ligier Mugen Honda	1:20.426
19	MARQUES	Minardi Ford	1:21.421
20	LAMY	Minardi Ford	1:21.491
21	BADOER	Forti Ford	1:23.174
22	MONTERMINI	Forti Ford	1:23.454

Race Results

POS	DRIVER	LAPS	GAP	TIME
1	HILL	71		1:49:52.976
2	ALESI	71	17.982	1:50:10.958
3	SCHUMACHER	70	1 lap	
4	HAKKINEN	70	1 lap	
5	SALO	70	1 lap	
6	PANIS	70	1 lap	
7	IRVINE	70	1 lap	
8	DINIZ	69	2 laps	
9	KATAYAMA	69	2 laps	
10	LAMY	68	3 laps	
11	BADOER	67	4 laps	

Drivers' Points

DRIVER	RACE PTS	TOTAL PTS
HILL	10	20
VILLENEUVE	0	6
ALESI	6	6
HAKKINEN	3	5
IRVINE	0	4
SCHUMACHER	4	4
BERGER	0	3
SALO	2	3
PANIS	1	1

Constructors' Points

CONSTRUCTOR	RACE PTS	TOTAL PTS
Williams Renault	10	26
Benetton Renault	6	9
Ferrari	4	8
McLaren Mercedes	3	5
Tyrrell Yamaha	2	3
Ligier Mugen Honda	1	1

Best Times

Winner's Speed:	Damon Hill		167.673 kph
Fastest Lap:	Damon Hill	1:21.547	190.932 kph

THE ARGENTINE GRAND PRIX
April 7, 1996

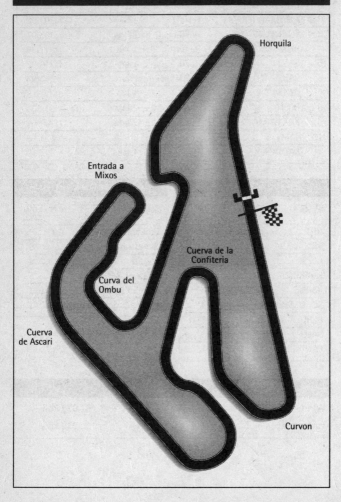

Horquila

Entrada a
Mixos

Cuerva de la
Confiteria

Curva del
Ombu

Cuerva
de Ascari

Curvon

Qualifying Times

POS	DRIVER	ENTRANT	TIME
1	HILL	Williams Renault	1:30.346
2	SCHUMACHER	Ferrari	1:30.598
3	VILLENEUVE	Williams Renault	1:30.907
4	ALESI	Benetton Renault	1:31.038
5	BERGER	Benetton Renault	1:31.262
6	BARRICHELLO	Jordan Peugeot	1:31.404
7	VERSTAPPEN	Footwork Hart	1:31.615
8	HAKKINEN	McLaren Mercedes	1:31.801
9	COULTHARD	McLaren Mercedes	1:32.001
10	IRVINE	Ferrari	1:32.058
11	FRENTZEN	Sauber Ford	1:32.130
12	PANIS	Ligier Mugen Honda	1:32.177
13	KATAYAMA	Tyrrell Yamaha	1:32.407
14	MARQUES	Minardi Ford	1:32.502
15	BRUNDLE	Jordan Peugeot	1:32.696
16	SALO	Tyrrell Yamaha	1:32.903
17	HERBERT	Sauber Ford	1:33.256
18	DINIZ	Ligier Mugen Honda	1:33.424
19	LAMY	Minardi Ford	1:33.727
20	ROSSET	Footwork Hart	1:33.752
21	BADOER	Forti Ford	1:34.830
22	MONTERMINI	Forti Ford	1:35.651

Race Results

POS	DRIVER	LAPS	GAP	TIME
1	HILL	72		1:54:55.322
2	VILLENEUVE	72	12.167	1:55:07.489
3	ALESI	72	14.754	1:55:10.076
4	BARRICHELLO	72	55.131	1:55:50.453
5	IRVINE	72	1:04.991	1:56:00.313
6	VERSTAPPEN	72	1:08.913	1:56:04.235
7	COULTHARD	72	1:13.400	1:56:08.722
8	PANIS	72	1:14.295	1:56:09.617

Drivers' Points

DRIVER	RACE PTS	TOTAL PTS
HILL	10	30
VILLENEUVE	6	12
ALESI	4	10
IRVINE	2	6
HAKKINEN	0	5
SCHUMACHER	0	4
BERGER	0	3
BARRICHELLO	0	3
SALO	0	3
PANIS	0	1
VERSTAPPEN	1	1

Constructors' Points

CONSTRUCTOR	RACE PTS	TOTAL PTS
Williams Renault	16	42
Benetton Renault	4	13
Ferrari	2	10
McLaren Mercedes	0	5
Jordan Peugeot	3	3
Tyrrell Yamaha	0	3
Footwork Hart	1	1
Ligier Mugen Honda	0	1

Best Times

Winner's Speed:	Damon Hill		160.013 kph
Fastest Lap:	Jean Alesi	1:29.413	171.478 kph

THE EUROPEAN GRAND PRIX
April 28, 1996

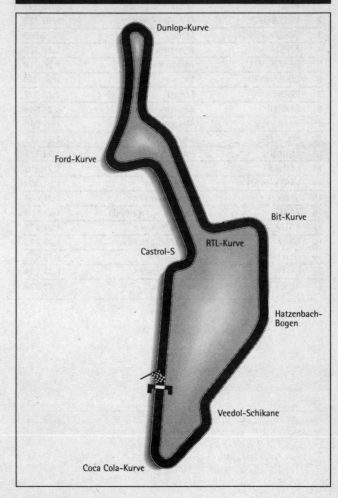

Dunlop-Kurve

Ford-Kurve

Bit-Kurve

RTL-Kurve

Castrol-S

Hatzenbach-Bogen

Veedol-Schikane

Coca Cola-Kurve

POS	DRIVER	ENTRANT	TIME
	Qualifying Times		
1	HILL	Williams Renault	1:18.941
2	VILLENEUVE	Williams Renault	1:19.721
3	SCHUMACHER	Ferrari	1:20.149
4	ALESI	Benetton Renault	1:20.711
5	BARRICHELLO	Jordan Peugeot	1:20.818
6	COULTHARD	McLaren Mercedes	1:20.888
7	IRVINE	Ferrari	1:20.931
8	BERGER	Benetton Renault	1:21.054
9	HAKKINEN	McLaren Mercedes	1:21.078
10	FRENTZEN	Sauber Ford	1:21.113
12	BRUNDLE	Jordan Peugeot	1:21.177
13	HERBERT	Sauber Ford	1:21.210
14	VERSTAPPEN	Arrows Hart	1:21.367
15	SALO	Tyrrell Yamaha	1:21.458
16	PANIS	Ligier Mugen Honda	1:21.509
17	KATAYAMA	Tyrrell Yamaha	1:21.812
18	DINIZ	Ligier Mugen Honda	1:22.733
19	FISICHELLA	Minardi Ford	1:22.921
20	LAMY	Minardi Ford	1:23.139
21	ROSSET	Arrows Hart	1:23.620

Race Results

POS	DRIVER	LAPS	GAP	TIME
1	VILLENEUVE	67		1:33:26.473
2	SCHUMACHER	67	0.762	1:33:27.235
3	COULTHARD	67	32.834	1:33:59.307
4	HILL	67	33.511	1:33:59.984
5	BARRICHELLO	67	33.713	1:34:00.186
6	BRUNDLE	67	55.567	1:34:22.040
7	HERBERT	67	1:18.027	1:34:44.500
8	HAKKINEN	67	1:18.438	1:34:44.911
9	BERGER	67	1:21.061	1:37:47.534
10	DINIZ	66	1 laps	
11	ROSSET	65	2 laps	
12	LAMY	65	2 laps	
13	FISICHELLA	65	2 laps	

Drivers' Points

DRIVER	RACE PTS	TOTAL PTS
HILL	3	33
VILLENEUVE	10	22
ALESI	0	10
SCHUMACHER	6	10
IRVINE	0	6
HAKKINEN	0	5
BARRICHELLO	2	5
COULTHARD	4	4
BERGER	0	3
SALO	0	3
PANIS	0	1
VERSTAPPEN	0	1
BRUNDLE	1	1

Constructors' Points

CONSTRUCTOR	RACE PTS	TOTAL PTS
Williams Renault	13	55
Ferrari	6	16
Benetton Renault	0	13
McLaren Mercedes	4	9
Jordan Peugeot	3	6
Tyrrell Yamaha	0	3
Ligier Mugen Honda	0	1
Footwork Hart	0	1

Best Times

Winner's Speed:
Jacques Villeneuve 196.006 kph

Fastest Lap:
Damon Hill 1:21.363, 201.585 kph

THE SAN MARINO GRAND PRIX
May 5, 1996

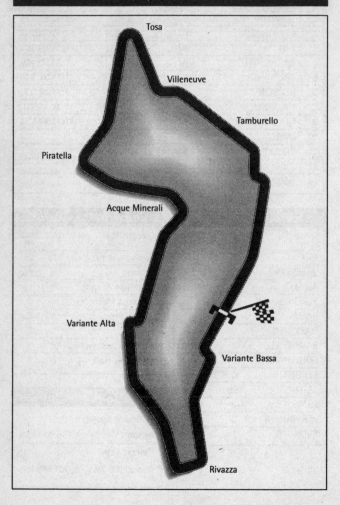

Tosa

Villeneuve

Tamburello

Piratella

Acque Minerali

Variante Alta

Variante Bassa

Rivazza

Qualifying Times

POS	DRIVER	ENTRANT	TIME
1	SCHUMACHER	Ferrari	1:26.890
2	HILL	Williams Renault	1:27.105
3	VILLENEUVE	Williams Renault	1:27.220
4	COULTHARD	McLaren Mercedes	1:27.688
5	ALESI	Benetton Renault	1:28.009
6	IRVINE	Ferrari	1:28.205
7	BERGER	Benetton Renault	1:28.336
8	SALO	Tyrrell Yamaha	1:28.423
9	BARRICHELLO	Jordan Peugeot	1:28.632
10	FRENTZEN	Sauber Ford	1:28.785
11	HAKKINEN	McLaren Mercedes	1:29.079
12	BRUNDLE	Jordan Peugeot	1:29.099
13	PANIS	Ligier Mugen Honda	1:29.472
14	VERSTAPPEN	Arrows Hart	1:29.539
15	HERBERT	Sauber Ford	1:29.541
16	KATAYAMA	Tyrrell Yamaha	1:29.892
17	DINIZ	Ligier Mugen Honda	1:29.989
18	LAMY	Minardi Ford	1:30.471
19	FISICHELLA	Minardi Ford	1:30.814
20	ROSSET	Arrows Hart	1:31.316
21	BADOER	Forti Ford	1:32.037

Race Results

POS	DRIVER	LAPS	GAP	TIME
1	HILL	63		1:35:26.156
2	SCHUMACHER	63	16.460	1:35:42.616
3	BERGER	63	46.891	1:36:13.047
4	IRVINE	63	1:01.583	1:36:27.739
5	BARRICHELLO	63	1:18.490	1:36:44.646
6	ALESI	62	1 lap	1:35:43.597
7	DINIZ	62	1 lap	1:36:33.333
8	HAKKINEN	61	DNF	1:34:49.164
9	LAMY	61	2 laps	1:36:59.418
10	BADOER	59	4 laps	1:36:10.706
11	VILLENEUEVE	57	DNF	1:27:49.134

Drivers' Points

DRIVER	RACE PTS	TOTAL PTS
HILL	10	43
VILLENEUVE	0	22
SCHUMACHER	6	16
ALESI	1	11
IRVINE	3	9
BERGER	4	7
BARRICHELLO	2	7
HAKKINEN	0	5
COULTHARD	0	4
SALO	0	3
PANIS	0	1
VERSTAPPEN	1	1
BRUNDLE	0	1

Constructors' Points

CONSTRUCTOR	RACE PTS	TOTAL PTS
Williams Renault	10	65
Ferrari	9	25
Benetton Renault	5	18
McLaren Mercedes	0	9
Jordan Peugeot	2	8
Tyrrell Yamaha	0	3
Ligier Mugen Honda	0	1
Footwork Hart	0	1

Best Times

Winner's Speed:	Damon Hill		193.761 kph
Fastest Lap:	Damon Hill	1:28.931	198.032 kph

THE MONACO GRAND PRIX
May 19, 1996

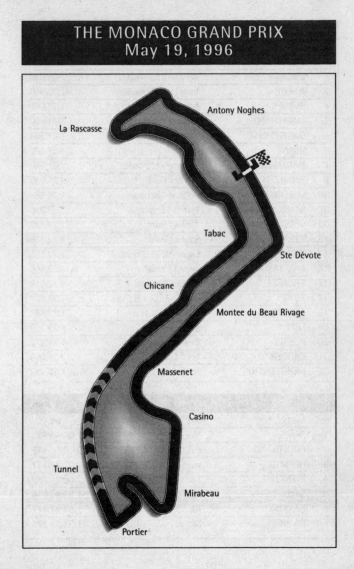

Qualifying Times

POS	DRIVER	ENTRANT	TIME
1	SCHUMACHER	Ferrari	1:20.356
2	HILL	Williams Renault	1:20.888
3	ALESI	Benetton Renault	1:20.918
4	BERGER	Benetton Renault	1:21.067
5	COULTHARD	McLaren Mercedes	1:21.460
6	BARRICHELLO	Jordan Peugeot	1:21.504
7	IRVINE	Ferrari	1:21.542
8	HAKKINEN	McLaren Mercedes	1:21.688
9	FRENTZEN	Sauber Ford	1:21.929
10	VILLENEUVE	Williams Renault	1:21.963
11	SALO	Tyrrell Yamaha	1:22.235
12	VERSTAPPEN	Arrows Hart	1:22.327
13	HERBERT	Sauber Ford	1:22.346
14	PANIS	Ligier Mugen Honda	1:22.358
15	KATAYAMA	Tyrrell Yamaha	1:22.460
16	BRUNDLE	Jordan Peugeot	1:22.519
17	DINIZ	Ligier Mugen Honda	1:22.682
18	FISICHELLA	Minardi Ford	1:22.684
19	LAMY	Minardi Ford	1:23.350
20	ROSSET	Arrows Hart	1:24.976
21	BADOER	Forti Ford	1:25.059
22	MONTERMINI	Forti Ford	1:25.393

Race Results

POS	DRIVER	LAPS	GAP	TIME
1	PANIS	75		2:00:45.629
2	COULTHARD	75	4.828	2:00:50.457
3	HERBERT	75	37.503	2:01:23.132
4	FRENTZEN	74	DNF	2:00:21.273
5	SALO	70	DNF	1:53:46.846
6	HAKKINEN	70	DNF	1:53:47.447
7	IRVINE	68	DNF	1:53:39.376

Drivers' Points

DRIVER	RACE PTS	TOTAL PTS
HILL	0	43
VILLENEUVE	0	22
SCHUMACHER	0	16
PANIS	10	11
ALESI	0	11
COULTHARD	6	10
IRVINE	0	9
BERGER	0	7
BARRICHELLO	0	7
HAKKINEN	1	6
SALO	2	5
HERBERT	4	4
FRENTZEN	3	3
VERSTAPPEN	0	1
BRUNDLE	0	1

Constructors' Points

CONSTRUCTOR	RACE PTS	TOTAL PTS
Williams Renault	0	65
Ferrari	0	25
Benetton Renault	0	18
McLaren Mercedes	7	16
Ligier Mugen Honda	10	11
Jordan Peugeot	0	8
Sauber Ford	7	7
Tyrrell Yamaha	2	5
Footwork Hart	2	1

Best Times

Winner's Speed:	Olivier Panis		124.014 kph
Fastest Lap:	Jean Alesi	1:25.205	140.611 kph

THE SPANISH GRAND PRIX
June 2, 1996

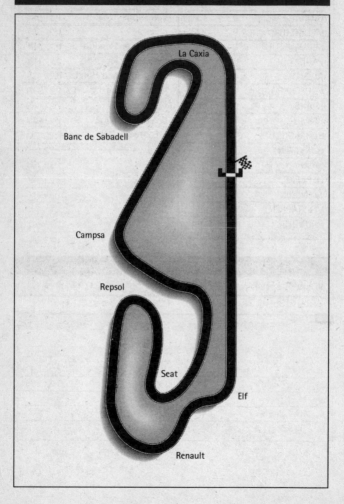

La Caxia

Banc de Sabadell

Campsa

Repsol

Seat

Elf

Renault

Qualifying Times

POS	DRIVER	ENTRANT	TIME
1	HILL	Williams Renault	1:20.650
2	VILLENEUVE	Williams Renault	1:21.084
3	SCHUMACHER	Ferrari	1:21.587
4	ALESI	Benetton Renault	1:22.061
5	BERGER	Benetton Renault	1:22.125
6	IRVINE	Ferrari	1:22.333
7	BARRICHELLO	Jordan Peugeot	1:22.379
8	PANIS	Ligier Mugen Honda	1:22.685
9	HERBERT	Sauber Ford	1:23.027
10	HAKKINEN	McLaren Mercedes	1:23.070
11	FRENTZEN	Sauber Ford	1:23.195
12	SALO	Tyrrell Yamaha	1:23.224
13	VERSTAPPEN	Arrows Hart	1:23.371
14	COULTHARD	McLaren Mercedes	1:23.416
15	BRUNDLE	Jordan Peugeot	1:23.438
16	KATAYAMA	Tyrrell Yamaha	1:24.401
17	DINIZ	Ligier Mugen Honda	1:24.468
18	LAMY	Minardi Ford	1:25.274
19	FISICHELLA	Minardi Ford	1:25.531
20	ROSSET	Arrows Hart	1:25.621

Race Results

POS	DRIVER	LAPS	GAP	TIME
1	SCHUMACHER	65		1:59:49.307
2	ALESI	65	45.302	2:00:34.609
3	VILLENEUVE	65	48.388	2:00:37.695
4	FRENTZEN	64	1 lap	
5	HAKKINEN	64	1 lap	
6	DINIZ	64	2 laps	

Drivers' Points

DRIVER	RACE PTS	TOTAL PTS
HILL	0	43
VILLENEUVE	4	26
SCHUMACHER	10	26
ALESI	6	17
PANIS	0	11
COULTHARD	0	10
IRVINE	0	9
HAKKINEN	2	8
BERGER	0	7
BARRICHELLO	0	7
FRENTZEN	3	6
SALO	0	5
HERBERT	0	4
BRUNDLE	0	1
VERSTAPPEN	0	1
DINIZ	1	1

Constructors' Points

CONSTRUCTOR	RACE PTS	TOTAL PTS
Williams Renault	4	69
Ferrari	10	35
Benetton Renault	6	24
McLaren Mercedes	2	18
Ligier Mugen Honda	1	12
Sauber Ford	3	10
Jordan Peugeot	0	8
Tyrrell Yamaha	0	5
Footwork Hart	0	1

Best Times

Winner's Speed: Michael Schumacher			153.785 kph
Fastest Lap: Schumacher	1:45.517	161.274 kph	

THE CANADIAN GRAND PRIX
June 16, 1996

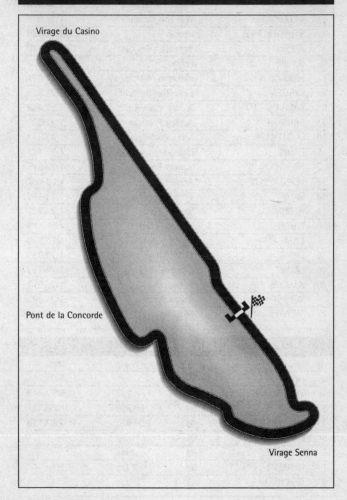

Virage du Casino

Pont de la Concorde

Virage Senna

Qualifying Times

POS	DRIVER	ENTRANT	TIME
1	HILL	Williams Renault	1:21.059
2	VILLENEUVE	Williams Renault	1:21.079
3	SCHUMACHER	Ferrari	1:21.196
4	ALESI	Benetton Renault	1:21.529
5	IRVINE	Ferrari	1:21.657
6	HAKKINEN	McLaren Mercedes	1:21.807
7	BERGER	Benetton Renault	1:21.926
8	BARRICHELLO	Jordan Peugeot	1:21.962
9	BRUNDLE	Jordan Peugeot	1:22.321
10	COULTHARD	McLaren Mercedes	1:22.332
11	PANIS	Ligier Mugen Honda	1:22.481
12	FRENTZEN	Sauber Ford	1:22.875
13	VERSTAPPEN	Arrows Hart	1:23.067
14	SALO	Tyrrell Yamaha	1:23.118
15	HERBERT	Sauber Ford	1:23.201
16	FISICHELLA	Minardi Ford	1:23.519
17	KATAYAMA	Tyrrell Yamaha	1:23.599
18	DINIZ	Ligier Mugen Honda	1:23.959
19	LAMY	Minardi Ford	1:24.262
20	BADOER	Forti Ford	1:25.012
21	ROSSET	Arrows Hart	1:25.193
22	MONTERMINI	Forti Ford	1:26.109

Race Results

POS	DRIVER	LAPS	GAP	TIME
1	HILL	69		1:36:03.465
2	VILLENEUVE	69	4.183	1:36:07.648
3	ALESI	69	54.656	1:36:58.121
4	COULTHARD	69	1:03.673	1:37:07.138
5	HAKKINEN	68	1 lap	
6	BRUNDLE	68	1 lap	
7	HERBERT	68	1 lap	
8	FISICHELLA	67	2 laps	

Drivers' Points

DRIVER	RACE PTS	TOTAL PTS
HILL	10	53
VILLENEUVE	6	32
SCHUMACHER	0	26
ALESI	4	21
COULTHARD	3	13
PANIS	0	11
HAKKINEN	2	10
IRVINE	0	9
BERGER	0	7
BARRICHELLO	0	7
FRENTZEN	0	6
SALO	0	5
HERBERT	0	4
BRUNDLE	1	2
VERSTAPPEN	0	1
DINIZ	0	1

Constructors' Points

CONSTRUCTOR	RACE PTS	TOTAL PTS
Williams Renault	16	85
Ferrari	0	35
Benetton Renault	7	28
McLaren Mercedes	3	23
Ligier Mugen Honda	0	12
Sauber Ford	0	10
Jordan Peugeot	0	9
Tyrrell Yamaha	0	5
Footwork Hart	0	1

Best Times

Winner's Speed: Damon Hill			190.541 kph
Fastest Lap:	Villeneuve	1:21.916	194.291kph

THE FRENCH GRAND PRIX
June 30, 1996

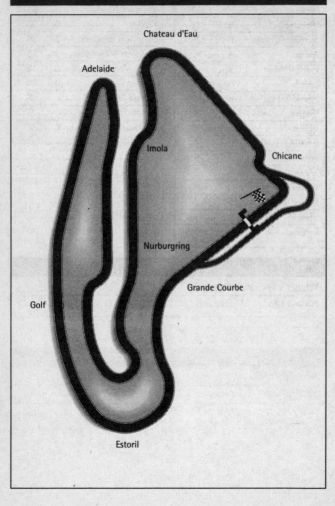

Chateau d'Eau

Adelaide

Imola

Chicane

Nurburgring

Grande Courbe

Golf

Estoril

Qualifying Times

POS	DRIVER	ENTRANT	TIME
1	SCHUMACHER	Ferrari	1:15.989
2	HILL	Williams Renault	1:16.058
3	ALESI	Benetton Renault	1:16.310
4	BERGER	Benetton Renault	1:16.592
5	HAKKINEN	McLaren Mercedes	1:16.634
6	VILLENEUVE	Williams Renault	1:16.905
7	COULTHARD	McLaren Mercedes	1:17.007
8	BRUNDLE	Jordan Peugeot	1:17.187
9	PANIS	Ligier Mugen Honda	1:17.390
10	BARRICHELLO	Jordan Peugeot	1:17.665
11	DINIZ	Ligier Mugen Honda	1:17.676
12	FRENTZEN	Sauber Ford	1:17.739
13	SALO	Tyrrell Yamaha	1:18.021
14	KATAYAMA	Tyrrell Yamaha	1:18.242
15	VERSTAPPEN	Arrows Hart	1:18.324
16	HERBERT	Sauber Ford	1:18.556
17	FISICHELLA	Minardi Ford	1:18.604
18	LAMY	Minardi Ford	1:19.210
19	ROSSET	Arrows Hart	1:19.242
20	BADOER	Forti Ford	1:20.562
21	MONTERMINI	Forti Ford	1:20.647
22	IRVINE	Ferrari	1:17.433

Best Times

Winner's Speed: Damon Hill		190.183 kph	
Fastest Lap:	Villeneuve	1:18.610	194.631 kph

Race Results

POS	DRIVER	LAPS	GAP	TIME
1	HILL	72		1:36:28.795
2	VILLENEUVE	72	8.127	1:36:36.922
3	ALESI	72	46.442	1:37:15.237
4	BERGER	72	46.859	1:37:15.654
5	HAKKINEN	72	1:02.774	1:37:31.569
6	COULTHARD	71	1 lap	
7	PANIS	71	1 lap	
8	BRUNDLE	71	1 lap	
9	BARRICHELLO	71	1 lap	
10	SALO	70	2 laps	
11	ROSSET	69	3 laps	
12	LAMY	69	3 laps	

Drivers' Points

DRIVER	RACE PTS	TOTAL PTS
HILL	10	63
VILLENEUVE	6	38
SCHUMACHER	0	26
ALESI	4	25
COULTHARD	1	14
HAKKINEN	2	12
PANIS	0	11
BERGER	3	10
IRVINE	0	9
BARRICHELLO	0	7
FRENTZEN	0	6
SALO	0	5
HERBERT	0	4
BRUNDLE	0	2
VERSTAPPEN	0	1
DINIZ	0	1

Constructors' Points

CONSTRUCTOR	RACE PTS	TOTAL PTS
Williams Renault	16	101
Ferrari	0	35
Benetton Renault	7	35
Marlboro McLaren Merc	3	26
Ligier Mugen Honda	0	12
Sauber Ford	0	10
Jordan Peugeot	0	9
Tyrrell Yamaha	0	5
Footwork Hart	1	1

THE BRITISH GRAND PRIX
July 14, 1996

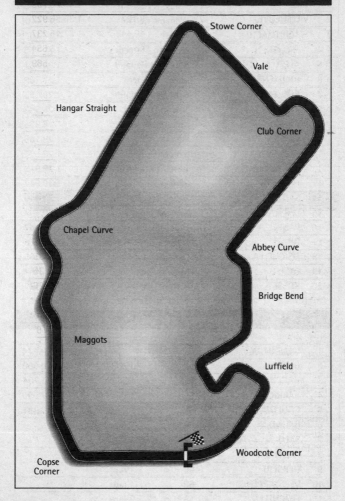

Stowe Corner

Vale

Hangar Straight

Club Corner

Chapel Curve

Abbey Curve

Bridge Bend

Maggots

Luffield

Woodcote Corner

Copse
Corner

Qualifying Times

POS	DRIVER	ENTRANT	TIME
1	HILL	Williams Renault	1:26.875
2	VILLENEUVE	Williams Renault	1:27.070
3	SCHUMACHER	Ferrari	1:27.707
4	HAKKINEN	McLaren Mercedes	1:27.856
5	ALESI	Benetton Renault	1:28.307
6	BARRICHELLO	Jordan Peugeot	1:28.409
7	BERGER	Benetton Renault	1:28.653
8	BRUNDLE	Jordan Peugeot	1:28.946
9	COULTHARD	McLaren Mercedes	1:28.966
10	IRVINE	Ferrari	1:29.186
11	FRENTZEN	Sauber Ford	1:29.591
12	KATAYAMA	Tyrrell Yamaha	1:29.913
13	HERBERT	Sauber Ford	1:29.947
14	SALO	Tyrrell Yamaha	1:29.949
15	VERSTAPPEN	Arrows Hart	1:30.102
16	PANIS	Ligier Mugen Honda	1:30.167
17	DINIZ	Ligier Mugen Honda	1:31.076
18	FISICHELLA	Minardi Ford	1:31.365
19	LAMY	Minardi Ford	1:31.454
20	ROSSET	Arrows Hart	1:30.529

Race Results

POS	DRIVER	LAPS	GAP	TIME
1	VILLENEUVE	61		1:33:00.874
2	BERGER	61	19.026	1:33:19.900
3	HAKKINEN	61	50.830	1:33:51.704
4	BARRICHELLO	61	1:06.716	1:34:07.590
5	COULTHARD	61	1:22.507	1:34:23.381
6	BRUNDLE	60	1 lap	
7	SALO	60	1 lap	
8	FRENTZEN	60	1 lap	
9	HERBERT	60	1 lap	
10	VERSTAPPEN	60	1 lap	
11	FISICHELLA	59	2 laps	

Drivers' Points

DRIVER	RACE PTS	TOTAL PTS
HILL	0	63
VILLENEUVE	10	48
SCHUMACHER	0	26
ALESI	0	25
COULTHARD	2	16
BERGER	6	16
HAKKINEN	4	16
PANIS	0	11
BARRICHELLO	3	10
IRVINE	0	9
FRENTZEN	0	6
SALO	0	5
HERBERT	0	4
BRUNDLE	1	3
VERSTAPPEN	0	1
DINIZ	0	1

Constructors' Points

CONSTRUCTOR	RACE PTS	TOTAL PTS
Williams Renault	10	111
Benetton Renault	6	41
Ferrari	0	35
McLaren Mercedes	6	32
Jordan Peugeot	4	13
Ligier Mugen Honda	0	12
Sauber Ford	0	10
Tyrrell Yamaha	0	5
Footwork Hart	0	1

Best Times

Winner's Speed:	Jacques Villeneuve		199.576 kph
Fastest Lap:	Villeneuve	1:29.288	204.497 kph

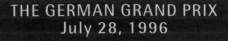

THE GERMAN GRAND PRIX
July 28, 1996

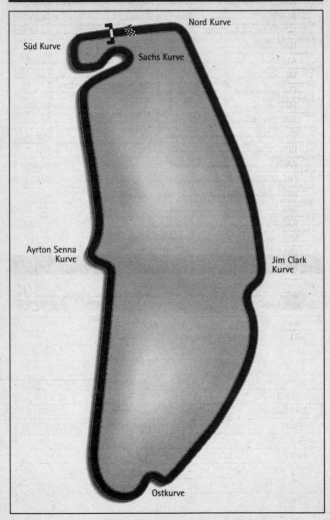

Nord Kurve

Süd Kurve

Sachs Kurve

Ayrton Senna
Kurve

Jim Clark
Kurve

Ostkurve

Qualifying Times

POS	DRIVER	ENTRANT	TIME
1	HILL	Williams Renault	1:43.912
2	BERGER	Benetton Renault	1:44.29
3	SCHUMACHER	Ferrari	1:44.477
4	HAKKINEN	McLaren Mercedes	1:44.644
5	ALESI	Benetton Renault	1:44.670
6	VILLENEUVE	Williams Renault	1:44.842
7	COULTHARD	McLaren Mercedes	1:44.951
8	IRVINE	Ferrari	1:45.389
9	BARRICHELLO	Jordan Peugeot	1:45.452
10	BRUNDLE	Jordan Peugeot	1:45.876
11	DINIZ	Ligier Mugen Honda	1:46.575
12	PANIS	Ligier Mugen Honda	1:46.746
13	FRENTZEN	Sauber Ford	1:46.899
14	HERBERT	Sauber Ford	1:47.711
15	SALO	Tyrrell Yamaha	1:48.139
16	KATAYAMA	Tyrrell Yamaha	1:48.381
17	VERSTAPPEN	Arrows Hart	1:48.512
18	LAMY	Minardi Ford	1:49.461
19	ROSSET	Arrows Hart	1:49.551

Race Results

POS	DRIVER	LAPS	GAP	TIME
1	HILL	45		1:21:43.417
2	ALESI	45	11.452	1:21:54.869
3	VILLENEUVE	45	33.926	1:22:17.343
4	SCHUMACHER	45	41.517	1:22:24.934
5	COULTHARD	45	42.196	1:22:25.613
6	BARRICHELLO	45	1:42.099	1:23:25.516
7	PANIS	45	1:43.912	1:23:27.329
8	FRENTZEN	44	1 lap	
9	SALO	44	1 lap	
10	BRUNDLE	44	1 lap	
11	ROSSET	44	1 lap	
12	LAMY	43	2 laps	

Drivers' Points

DRIVER	RACE PTS	TOTAL PTS
HILL	10	73
VILLENEUVE	4	52
ALESI	6	31
SCHUMACHER	3	29
COULTHARD	2	18
BERGER	0	16
HAKKINEN	0	16
PANIS	0	11
BARRICHELLO	1	11
IRVINE	0	9
FRENTZEN	0	6
SALO	0	5
HERBERT	0	4
BRUNDLE	0	3
VERSTAPPEN	0	1
DINIZ	0	1

Constructors' Points

CONSTRUCTOR	RACE PTS	TOTAL PTS
Williams Renault	14	125
Benetton Renault	6	47
Ferrari	3	38
McLaren Mercedes	2	34
Jordan Peugeot	1	14
Ligier Mugen Honda	0	12
Sauber Ford	0	10
Tyrrell Yamaha	0	5
Footwork Hart	0	1

Best Times

Winner's Speed:	Damon Hill	225.369 kph
Fastest Lap:	Damon Hill	1:46.504 230.280 kph

THE HUNGARIAN GRAND PRIX
August 11, 1996

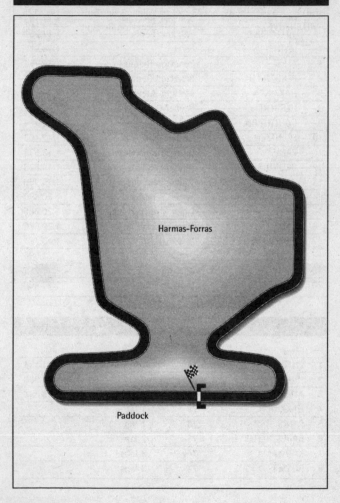

Harmas-Forras

Paddock

Qualifying Times

POS	DRIVER	ENTRANT	TIME
1	SCHUMACHER	Ferrari	1:17.129
2	HILL	Williams Renault	1:17.182
3	VILLENEUVE	Williams Renault	1:17.259
4	IRVINE	Ferrari	1:18.617
5	ALESI	Benetton Renault	1:18.754
6	BERGER	Benetton Renault	1:18.794
7	HAKKINEN	McLaren Mercedes	1:19.116
8	HERBERT	Sauber Ford	1:19.292
9	COULTHARD	McLaren Mercedes	1:19.384
10	FRENTZEN	Sauber Ford	1:19.463
11	PANIS	Ligier Mugen Honda	1:19.538
12	BRUNDLE	Jordan Peugeot	1:19.828
13	BARRICHELLO	Jordan Peugeot	1:19.966
14	KATAYAMA	Tyrrell Yamaha	1:20.499
15	DINIZ	Ligier Mugen Honda	1:20.665
16	SALO	Tyrrell Yamaha	1:20.678
17	VERSTAPPEN	Arrows Hart	1:20.781
18	ROSSET	Arrows Hart	1:21.590
19	LAMY	Minardi Ford	1:21.713
20	LAVAGGI	Minardi Ford	1:22.468

Race Results

POS	DRIVER	LAPS	GAP	TIME
1	VILLENEUVE	77		1:46:21.134
2	HILL	77	0.771	1:46:21.905
3	ALESI	77	1:24.212	1:47:45.346
4	HAKKINEN	76	1 lap	
5	PANIS	76	1 lap	
6	BARRICHELLO	75	2 laps	
7	KATAYAMA	74	3 laps	
8	ROSSET	74	3 laps	

Drivers' Points

DRIVER	RACE PTS	TOTAL PTS
HILL	6	79
VILLENEUVE	10	62
ALESI	4	35
SCHUMACHER	0	29
HAKKINEN	3	19
COULTHARD	0	18
BERGER	0	16
PANIS	2	13
BARRICHELLO	1	12
IRVINE	0	9
FRENTZEN	0	6
SALO	0	5
HERBERT	0	4
BRUNDLE	0	3
VERSTAPPEN	0	1
DINIZ	0	1

Constructors' Points

CONSTRUCTOR	RACE PTS	TOTAL PTS
Williams Renault	16	141
Benetton Renault	4	51
Ferrari	0	38
McLaren Mercedes	3	37
Jordan Peugeot	1	15
Ligier Mugen Honda	2	14
Sauber Ford	0	10
Tyrrell Yamaha	0	5
Arrows Hart	0	1

Best Times

Winner's Speed:	Jacques Villeneuve	172.316 kph
Fastest Lap:	Hill	1:20.093 178.293 kph

THE BELGIAN GRAND PRIX
August 25, 1996

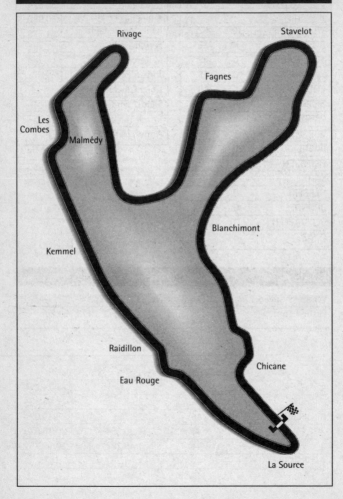

Rivage

Stavelot

Fagnes

Les
Combes

Malmédy

Blanchimont

Kemmel

Raidillon

Chicane

Eau Rouge

La Source

Qualifying Times

POS	DRIVER	ENTRANT	TIME
1	VILLENEUVE	Williams Renault	1:50.574
2	HILL	Williams Renault	1:50.980
3	SCHUMACHER	Ferrari	1:51.778
4	COULTHARD	McLaren Mercedes	1:51.884
5	BERGER	Benetton Renault	1:51.960
6	HAKKINEN	McLaren Mercedes	1:52.318
7	ALESI	Benetton Renault	1:52.354
8	BRUNDLE	Jordan Peugeot	1:52.977
9	IRVINE	Ferrari	1:53.043
10	BARRICHELLO	Jordan Peugeot	1:53.152
11	FRENTZEN	Sauber Ford	1:53.199
12	HERBERT	Sauber Ford	1:53.993
13	SALO	Tyrrell Yamaha	1:54.095
14	PANIS	Ligier Mugen Honda	1:54.220
15	DINIZ	Ligier Mugen Honda	1:54.700
16	VERSTAPPEN	Arrows Hart	1:55.150
17	KATAYAMA	Tyrrell Yamaha	1:55.371
18	ROSSET	Arrows Hart	1:56.286
19	LAMY	Minardi Ford	1:56.830

Race Results

POS	DRIVER	LAPS	GAP	TIME
1	SCHUMACHER	44		1:28:15.125
2	VILLENEUVE	44	5.602	1:28:20.727
3	HAKKINEN	44	15.710	1:28:30.835
4	ALESI	44	19.125	1:28:34.250
5	HILL	44	29.179	1:28:44.304
6	BERGER	44	29.896	1:28:45.021
7	SALO	44	1:00.754	1:29:15.879
8	KATAYAMA	44	1:40.227	1:29:55.352
9	ROSSET	43	1 lap	
10	LAMY	43	1 lap	

Drivers' Points

DRIVER	RACE PTS	TOTAL PTS
HILL	2	81
VILLENEUVE	6	68
SCHUMACHER	10	39
ALESI	3	38
HAKKINEN	4	23
COULTHARD	0	18
BERGER	1	17
PANIS	0	13
BARRICHELLO	0	12
IRVINE	0	9
FRENTZEN	0	6
SALO	0	5
HERBERT	0	4
BRUNDLE	0	3
VERSTAPPEN	0	1
DINIZ	0	1

Constructors' Points

CONSTRUCTOR	RACE PTS	TOTAL PTS
Williams Renault	8	149
Benetton Renault	4	55
Ferrari	10	48
McLaren Mercedes	4	41
Jordan Peugeot	0	15
Ligier Mugen Honda	0	14
Sauber Ford	0	10
Tyrrell Yamaha	0	5
Arrows Hart	0	1

Best Times

Winner's Speed: Michael Schumacher	208.374 kph		
Fastest Lap: Berger	1:53.067	221.783 kph	

THE ITALIAN GRAND PRIX
September 11, 1996

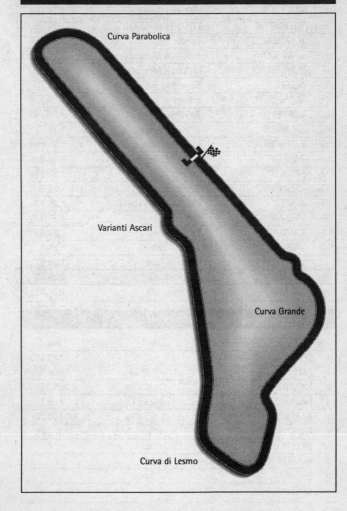

Curva Parabolica

Varianti Ascari

Curva Grande

Curva di Lesmo

Qualifying Times

POS	DRIVER	ENTRANT	TIME
1	HILL	Williams Renault	1:24.204
2	VILLENEUVE	Williams Renault	1:24.521
3	SCHUMACHER	Ferrari	1:24.781
4	HAKKINEN	McLaren Mercedes	1:24.939
5	COULTHARD	McLaren Mercedes	1:24.976
6	ALESI	Benetton Renault	1:25.201
7	IRVINE	Ferrari	1:25.226
8	BERGER	Benetton Renault	1:25.470
9	BRUNDLE	Jordan Peugeot	1:26.037
10	BARRICHELLO	Jordan Peugeot	1:26.194
11	PANIS	Ligier Mugen Honda	1:26.206
12	HERBERT	Sauber Ford	1:26.345
13	FRENTZEN	Sauber Ford	1:26.505
14	DINIZ	Ligier Mugen Honda	1:26.726
15	VERSTAPPEN	Arrows Hart	1:27.270
16	KATAYAMA	Tyrrell Yamaha	1:28.234
17	SALO	Tyrrell Yahama	1:28.472
18	LAMY	Minardi Ford	1:28.933
19	ROSSET	Arrows Hart	1:29.181
20	LAVAGGI	Minardi Ford	1:29.833

Race Results

POS	DRIVER	LAPS	GAP	TIME
1	SCHUMACHER	53		1:17:43.632
2	ALESI	53	18.265	1:18:01.897
3	HAKKINEN	53	1:06.635	1:18:50.267
4	BRUNDLE	53	1:25.217	1:19:08.849
5	BARRICHELLO	53	1:25.475	1:19:09.107
6	DINIZ	52	1 lap	
7	VILLENEUVE	52	1 lap	
8	VERSTAPPEN	52	1 lap	
9	HERBERT	51	2 laps	
10	KATAYAMA	51	2 laps	

Drivers' Points

DRIVER	RACE PTS	TOTAL PTS
HILL	0	81
VILLENEUVE	0	68
SCHUMACHER	10	49
ALESI	6	44
HAKKINEN	4	27
COULTHARD	0	18
BERGER	0	17
BARRICHELLO	2	14
PANIS	0	13
IRVINE	0	9
FRENTZEN	0	6
BRUNDLE	3	6
SALO	0	5
HERBERT	0	4
DINIZ	1	2
VERSTAPPEN	0	1

Constructors' Points

CONSTRUCTOR	RACE PTS	TOTAL PTS
Williams Renault	0	149
Benetton Renault	6	61
Ferrari	10	58
McLaren Mercedes	4	45
Jordan Peugeot	5	20
Ligier Mugen Honda	1	15
Sauber Ford	0	10
Tyrrell Yamaha	0	5
Arrows Hart	0	1

Best Times

Winner's Speed:	Michael Schumacher		235.957 kph
Fastest Lap:	Schumacher	1:26.110	241.147 kph

THE PORTUGUESE GRAND PRIX
September 22, 1996

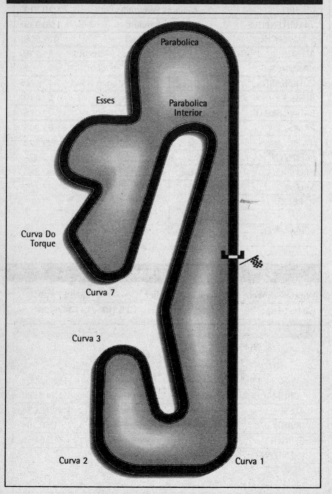

Qualifying Times

POS	DRIVER	ENTRANT	TIME
1	HILL	Williams Renault	1:20.330
2	VILLENEUVE	Williams Renault	1:20.339
3	ALESI	Benetton Renault	1:21.008
4	SCHUMACHER	Ferrari	1:21.236
5	BERGER	Benetton Renault	1:21.293
6	IRVINE	Ferrari	1:21.362
7	HAKKINEN	McLaren Mercedes	1:21.640
8	COULTHARD	McLaren Mercedes	1:22.066
9	BARRICHELLO	Jordan Peugeot	1:22.205
10	BRUNDLE	Jordan Peugeot	1:22.324
11	FRENTZEN	Sauber Ford	1:22.325
12	HERBERT	Sauber Ford	1:22.655
13	SALO	Tyrrell Yamaha	1:22.765
14	KATAYAMA	Tyrrell Yamaha	1:23.013
15	PANIS	Ligier Mugen Honda	1:23.055
16	VERSTAPPEN	Arrows Hart	1:23.531
17	ROSSET	Arrows Hart	1:24.230
18	DINIZ	Ligier Mugen Honda	1:24.293
19	LAMY	Minardi Ford	1:24.510
20	LAVAGGI	Minardi Ford	1:25.612

Race Results

POS	DRIVER	LAPS	GAP	TIME
1	VILLENEUVE	70		1:40:22.915
2	HILL	70	19.966	1:40:42.881
3	SCHUMACHER	70	53.765	1:41:16.680
4	ALESI	70	55.109	1:41:18.024
5	IRVINE	70	1:27.389	1:41:50.304
6	BERGER	70	1:33.141	1:41:56.056
7	FRENTZEN	69	1 lap	
8	HERBERT	69	1 lap	

contd over page

Race Results continued

POS	DRIVER	LAPS	GAP	TIME
9	BRUNDLE	69	1 lap	
10	PANIS	69	1 lap	
11	SALO	69	1 lap	
12	KATAYAMA	68	2 laps	
13	COULTHARD	68	2 laps	
14	ROSSET	67	3 laps	
15	LAVAGGI	65	5 laps	
16	LAMY	65	5 laps	

Constructors' Points

CONSTRUCTOR	RACE PTS	TOTAL PTS
Williams Renault	16	165
Benetton Renault	4	65
Ferrari	6	64
McLaren Mercedes	0	45
Jordan Peugeot	0	20
Ligier Mugen Honda	0	15
Sauber Ford	0	10
Tyrrell Yamaha	0	5
Arrows Hart	0	1

Drivers' Points

DRIVER	RACE PTS	TOTAL PTS
HILL	6	87
VILLENEUVE	10	78
SCHUMACHER	4	53
ALESI	3	47
HAKKINEN	0	27
BERGER	1	18
COULTHARD	0	18
BARRICHELLO	0	14
PANIS	0	13
IRVINE	2	11
FRENTZEN	0	6
BRUNDLE	0	6
SALO	0	5
HERBERT	0	4
DINIZ	0	2
VERSTAPPEN	0	1

Best Times

Winner's Speed:	Jacques Villeneuve		182.423 kph
Fastest Lap:	Villeneuve	1:22.873	189.398 kph

THE JAPANESE GRAND PRIX
October 13, 1996

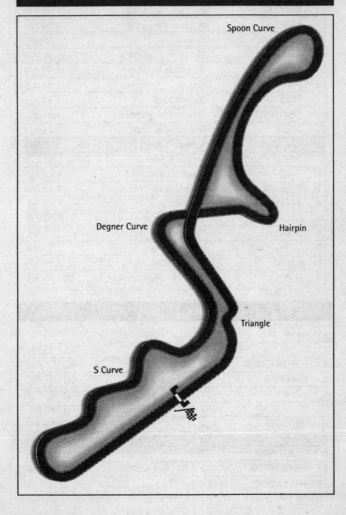

Spoon Curve

Degner Curve

Hairpin

Triangle

S Curve

Qualifying Times

POS	DRIVER	ENTRANT	TIME
1	VILLENEUVE	Williams Renault	1:38.909
2	HILL	Wiliams Renault	1:39.370
3	SCHUMACHER	Ferrari	1:40.071
4	BERGER	Benetton Renault	1:40.364
5	HAKKINEN	Benetton Renault	1:40.458
6	IRVINE	Ferrari	1:41.005
7	FRENTZEN	Sauber Ford	1:41.277
8	COULTHARD	McLaren Mercedes	1:41.384
9	ALESI	Benetton Renault	1:41.562
10	BRUNDLE	Jordan Peugeot	1:41.660
11	BARRICHELLO	Jordan Peugeot	1:41.919
12	PANIS	Ligier Mugen Honda	1:42.206
13	HERBERT	Sauber Ford	1:42.658
14	KATAYAMA	Minardi Ford	1:42.711
15	SALO	Tyrrell Yamaha	1:42.840
16	DINIZ	Ligier Mugen Honda	1:43.196
17	VERSTAPPEN	Footwork Hart	1:43.386
18	LAMY	Minardi Ford	1:44.874
19	ROSSET	Footwork Hart	1:45.412

Race Results

POS	DRIVER	LAPS	GAP	TIME
1	HILL	52		1:32:33.791
2	SCHUMACHER	52	1.883	1:32:35.674
3	HAKKINEN	52	3.212	1:32:37.003
4	BERGER	52	26.526	1:33:00.317
5	BRUNDLE	52	1:07.120	1:33:40.911
6	FRENTZEN	52	1:21.186	1:33:54.977
7	PANIS	52	1:24.510	1:33:58.301
8	COULTHARD	52	1:25.233	1:33:59.024
9	BARRICHELLO	52	1:41.065	1:34:14.856

continued over page

Race Results continued

POS	DRIVER	LAPS	GAP	TIME
10	HERBERT	52	1:41.799	1:34:15.590
11	VERSTAPPEN	51	1 lap	
12	LAMY	50	2 laps	
13	ROSSET	50	2 laps	

Drivers' Points

DRIVER	RACE PTS	TOTAL PTS
HILL	10	97
VILLENEUVE	0	78
SCHUMACHER	6	59
ALESI	0	47
HAKKINEN	4	31
BERGER	3	21
COULTHARD	0	18
BARRICHELLO	0	14
PANIS	0	13
IRVINE	0	11
BRUNDLE	2	8
FRENTZEN	1	7
SALO	0	5
HERBERT	0	4
DINIZ	0	2
VERSTAPPEN	0	1

Constructors' Points

CONSTRUCTOR	RACE PTS	TOTAL PTS
Williams Renault	10	175
Ferrari	6	70
Benetton Renault	3	68
McLaren Mercedes	4	49
Jordan Peugeot	2	22
Ligier Mugen Honda	0	15
Sauber Ford	1	11
Tyrrell Yamaha	0	5
Footwork Hart	0	1

Best Times

Winner's Speed:	Damon Hill		197.520 kph
Fastest Lap:	Villeneuve	1:44.043	202.900 kph

THE AUSTRALIAN GRAND PRIX
March 9, 1997

For race course map, see page 204.

Qualifying Times

POS	DRIVER	ENTRANT	TIME
1	VILLENEUVE	Williams Renault	1:29.369
2	FRENTZEN	Williams Renault	1:31.123
3	M SCHUMACHER	Ferrari	1:31.472
4	COULTHARD	McLaren Mercedes	1:31.531
5	IRVINE	Ferrari	1:31.881
6	HÄKKINEN	McLaren Mercedes	1:31.971
7	HERBERT	Sauber Petronas	1:32.287
8	ALESI	Benetton Renault	1:32.593
9	PANIS	Prost Mugen Honda	1:32.842
10	BERGER	Benetton Renault	1:32.870
11	BARRICHELLO	Stewart Ford	1:33.075
12	R SCHUMACHER	Jordan Peugeot	1:33.130
13	LARINI	Sauber Petronas	1:33.327
14	FISICHELLA	Jordan Peugeot	1:33.552
15	KATAYAMA	Minardi Hart	1:33.798
16	NAKANO	Prost Mugen Honda	1:33.989
17	TRULLI	Minardi Hart	1:34.120
18	SALO	Tyrell Ford	1:34.229
19	MAGNUSSEN	Stewart Ford	1:34.623
20	HILL	Arrows Yamaha	1:34.806
21	VERSTAPPEN	Tyrell Ford	1:34.943
22	DINIZ	Arrows Yamaha	1:35.972

Race Results

POS	DRIVER	LAPS	GAP	TIME
1	COULTHARD	58		1:30:28.718
2	M SCHUMACHER	58	20.046	1:30:48.764
3	HÄKKINEN	58	22.177	1:30:50.895
4	BERGER	58	22.841	1:30:51.559
5	PANIS	58	1:00.308	1:31.29.026
6	LARINI	58	1:36.040	1:32:04.758
7	NAKANO	56	2 laps	
8	TRULLI	55	3 laps	
9	DINIZ	54	4 laps	

Constructors' Points

CONSTRUCTOR	RACE PTS	TOTAL PTS
McLaren Mercedes	14	14
Ferrari	6	6
Benetton Renault	3	3
Prost Mugen Honda	2	2
Sauber Petronas	1	1

Drivers' Points

DRIVER	RACE PTS	TOTAL PTS
COULTHARD	10	10
M SCHUMACHER	6	6
HÄKKINEN	4	4
BERGER	3	3
PANIS	2	2
LARINI	1	1

Best Times

Winner's Speed:	David Coulthard		203.926 kph
Fastest Lap:	H H Frentzen	1:30.585	210.710 kph

THE BRAZILIAN GRAND PRIX
March 30, 1997

For race course map, see page 207.

Qualifying Times

POS	DRIVER	ENTRANT	TIME
1	VILLENEUVE	Williams Renault	1:16.004
2	M SCHUMACHER	Ferrari	1:16.594
3	BERGER	Benetton Renault	1:16.644
4	HÄKKINEN	McLaren Mercedes	1:16.692
5	PANIS	Prost Mugen Honda	1:16.756
6	ALESI	Benetton Renault	1:16.757
7	FISICHELLA	Jordan Peugeot	1:16.912
8	FRENTZEN	Williams Renault	1:16.971
9	HILL	Arrows Yamaha	1:17.090
10	R SCHUMACHER	Jordan Peugeot	1:17.175
11	BARRICHELLO	Stewart Ford	1:17.259
12	COULTHARD	McLaren Mercedes	1:17.527
13	HERBERT	Sauber Petronas	1:17.409
14	IRVINE	Ferrari	1:17.527
15	NAKANO	Prost Mugen Honda	1:17.999
16	DINIZ	Arrows Yamaha	1:18.095
17	TRULLI	Minardi Hart	1:18.336
18	KATAYAMA	Minardi Hart	1:18.557
19	LARINI	Sauber Petronas	1:18.644
20	MAGNUSSEN	Stewart Ford	1:18.773
21	VERSTAPPEN	Tyrell Ford	1:18.885
22	SALO	Tyrell Ford	1:19.274

Best Times

Winner's Speed:	Jacques Villeneuve		192.905 kph
Fastest Lap:	Jacques Villeneuve	1:18.397	197.809 kph

Race Results

POS	DRIVER	LAPS	GAP	TIME
1	VILLENEUVE	72		1:36:06.990
2	BERGER	72	4.190	1:36:11.180
3	PANIS	72	15.870	1:36:22.860
4	HÄKKINEN	72	33.033	1:36:40.023
5	M SCHUMACHER	72	33.731	1:36:40.721
6	ALESI	72	34.020	1:36:41.010
7	HERBERT	72	50.912	1:36:57.902
8	FISICHELLA	72	1:00.639	1:37:07.629
9	FRENTZEN	72	1:15.402	1:37:22.392
10	COULTHARD	71	1 lap	
11	LARINI	71	1 lap	
12	TRULLI	71	1 lap	
13	SALO	71	1 lap	
14	NAKANO	71	1 lap	
15	VERSTAPPEN	70	2 laps	
16	IRVINE	70	2 laps	
17	HILL	DNF		
18	KATAYAMA	67	5 laps	

Constructors' Points

CONSTRUCTOR	RACE PTS	TOTAL PTS
McLaren Mercedes	17	31
Williams Renault	10	10
Benetton Renault	10	13
Ferrari	8	14
Prost Mugen Honda	6	8
Sauber Petronas	1	2

Drivers' Points

DRIVER	RACE PTS	TOTAL PTS
COULTHARD	10	10
VILLENEUVE	0	10
BERGER	6	9
M SCHUMACHER	2	8
HÄKKINEN	3	7
PANIS	4	6
LARINI	0	1
ALESI	1	1

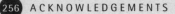

ACKNOWLEDGEMENTS

HarperCollins*Publishers* would like to thank:
Rothmans Racing Limited,
Belinda Olins and Fiona McWhirter at FJ Associates,
Marie-Claude Libault at Rothmans for picture research,
Tyrrell Yamaha and Avenue Communications Limited for
the lap simulation and track reference,
Kim Jarvis at ICN Promocourse for race results
(Race results ©1996 Fédération International de
l'Automobile, 8 Place de la Concorde, Paris, 75008 France),
Formula One Constructors Association for permission
to reproduce race results,
Arthur Brown, Peter Cooling and Alistair Plumb
at Cooling Brown.

ARTISTS

Greg Whyte and Russell Lewis.

PICTURE CREDITS

Agence DPPI: colour plates section pp 9, 10.
Allsport: 16.
Empics: 4, 5 top and bottom, 10 middle, 11 top and middle,
12, 14 top and bottom, 15 bottom, 16 top and bottom.
ICN: 2, 3 top, 6, 7, 8, 14 middle.
Rothmans: 3 middle, 13 top.
Sutton Images: 11 bottom, 15 top and middle.
Sygma: 1, 3 bottom, 4 top, 10 top, 15 middle.